the ANTIQUE DEALERS pocketbook

©

Lyle Publications · 1972

While every care has been taken in compiling the information contained in these volumes the publishers cannot accept any liability for loss, financial or otherwise, incurred by reliance placed on the information herein.

First Edition February 1972

Lyle Publications

7 LIVERPOOL TERRACE, WORTHING, SUSSEX.

phone Worthing 36373

CONTENTS

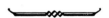

INTRODUCTION

With the ever increasing popularity of antique collecting, the need has arisen for a comprehensive reference book containing detailed illustrations - not only of the items which command the highest prices but also those pieces which, although not antiques in the true sense, are much sought after by members of the trade.

Here, in one handy, pocket sized volume, are well over 2,000 clear illustrations to facilitate instant recognition and dating of the host of day to day items which make up the bulk of the antique market.

Compiled primarily with the professional dealer in view, this book makes inter-trade reference simple and accurate. Used to full advantage it can hardly fail to greatly increase turnover.

Every professional antique dealer is aware of the frustration and waste of valuable time resulting from hopelessly inaccurate descriptions of items offered by casual callers - on these pages may be found an illustration which, if not exactly tallying in every detail with the offered item, will be, in most cases close enough to enable the dealer to judge whether or not it will be worth his while to call.

At last an end may be put to confusing (and confused) descriptions between dealer and dealer and between shipper and supplier - you need only refer to the page and reference number to ensure that the right information is being passed.

Interior decorators too, will find communication with their clients considerably improved through use of this book, once again ensuring that there can be no confusion resulting from verbal descriptions being inaccurately given or incompletely understood.

We are confident that every user of The Antique Dealer's Pocket Book will find it of invaluable assistance in the smooth running of his business and a useful addition to his works of reference.

R. A. CURTIS

Printed in Great Britain by

CORMORANT PRESS LTD
MEADOW ROAD INDUSTRIAL ESTATE
WORTHING SUSSEX ENGLAND

MONARCHS

HENRY 1V	1399 - 1413
HENRY V	1413 - 1422
HENRY V1	1422 - 1461
EDWARD 1V	1461 - 1483
EDWARD V	1483 - 1483
RICHARD 111	1483 - 1485
HENRY V11	1485 - 1509
HENRY V111	1509 - 1547
EDWARD V1	1547 - 1553
MARY	1553 - 1558
ELIZABETH	1558 - 1603
JAMES 1	1603 - 1625
CHARLES 1	1625 - 1649
COMMONWEALTH	1649 - 1660
CHARLES 11	1660 - 1685
JAMES 11	1685 - 1689
WILLIAM & MARY	1689 - 1695
WILLIAM 111	1695 - 1702
ANNE	1702 - 1714
GEORGE 1	1714 - 1727
GEORGE 11	1727 - 1760
GEORGE 111	1760 - 1820
GEORGE 1V	1820 - 1830
WILLIAM 1V	1830 - 1837
VICTORIA	1837 - 1901
EDWARD V11	1901 - 1910

PERIODS

TUDOR PERIOD	.. ..	1485 - 1603
ELIZABETHAN PERIOD	.. ..	1558 - 1603
INIGO JONES "	.. ..	1572 - 1652
JACOBEAN PERIOD	.. ..	1603 - 1688
STUART PERIOD	.. ..	1603 - 1714
A. C. BOULLE	.. ..	1642 - 1732
LOUIS XIV PERIOD	.. ..	1643 - 1715
GRINLING GIBBONS	.. ..	1648 - 1726
CROMWELLIAN PERIOD	.. ..	1649 - 1660
CAROLEAN PERIOD	.. ..	1660 - 1685
WILLIAM KENT	.. ..	1684 - 1748
WILLIAM & MARY PERIOD	.. ..	1689 - 1702
QUEEN ANNE PERIOD	.. ..	1702 - 1714
GEORGIAN PERIOD	.. ..	1714 - 1820
T. CHIPPENDALE	.. ..	1715 - 1762
LOUIS XV PERIOD	.. ..	1723 - 1774
A. HEPPLEWHITE	.. ..	1727 - 1788
ADAM PERIOD	.. ..	1728 - 1792
ANGELICA KAUFMANN	.. ..	1741 - 1807
T. SHERATON	.. ..	1751 - 1806
LOUIS XVI	.. ..	1774 - 1793
T. SHEARER	.. ..	(circa) 1780
REGENCY PERIOD	.. ..	1800 - 1830
EMPIRE PERIOD	.. ..	1804 - 1815
VICTORIAN PERIOD	.. ..	1830 - 1901
EDWARDIAN PERIOD	.. ..	1901 - 1910

REGISTRY OF DESIGNS

USED 1842 to 1883

BELOW ARE ILLUSTRATED THE TWO FORMS OF 'REGISTRY OF DESIGN' MARK USED BETWEEN THE YEARS OF 1842 TO 1883.

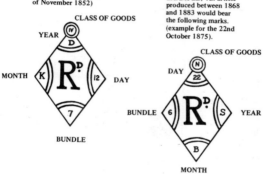

EXAMPLE: An article produced between 1842 and 1867 would bear the following marks. (example for the 12th of November 1852)

EXAMPLE; An article produced between 1868 and 1883 would bear the following marks. (example for the 22nd October 1875).

DATE AND LETTER CODE

JANUARY	C	1842	X	54	J	66	Q	78	D
FEBRUARY	G	43	H	55	E	67	T	79	Y
MARCH	W	44	C	56	L	68	X	80	J
APRIL	H	45	A	57	K	69	H	81	E
MAY	E	46	I	58	B	70	O	82	L
JUNE	M	47	F	59	M	71	A	83	K
JULY	I	48	U	60	Z	72	I		
AUGUST	R	49	S	61	R	73	F		
SEPTEMBER	D	50	V	62	O	74	U		
OCTOBER	B	51	P	63	G	75	S		
NOVEMBER	K	52	D	64	N	76	V		
DECEMBER	A	53	Y	65	W	77	P		

CHINA MARKS

BELLEEK
1857 onwards

BOW
1750-1776

1750   1760   1770

CAUGHLEY
1772-1814

imitation
Worcester   in blue   in blue   impressed

SALOPIAN

CHELSEA
1745-1784

Chelsea 1745
incised
1745-1749

in relief
1750-1753

red
1755

gold
1758-1770

COLEBROOK DALE
1785-1820

C D ale.   Coalport
1785-1820

COPELAND
1847

COPELAND & GARRETT
1833

1847   1847-1891   1833-1847

DAVENPORT
1793-1882

Davenport

DAVENPORT
LONGPORT
STAFFORDSHIRE

DAVENPORTS
STONE CHINA

DERBY
1745 onwards

1750   1760   1770-1780

DOULTON
1815

pre 1836   1872

FRANKENTHAL
1755-1800

blue
1756

blue
1756-1759

blue
1762-1793

blue
1771

HOCHST
1750-1798

red
1750-1762

blue
1762-1796

1765-1774

impressed
1760-1765

LEEDS
1760-1878

Hartley, Greens & Co
LEEDS POTTERY
1760-1783

LEEDS POTTERY
LEEDS POTTERY
impressed 1864

MARTIN BROS
1873-1915

Martin Bros
London & Southall
1873

R.W. MARTIN & BROS
1900

MASONS
1795-1854

MASONS
PATENT IRONSTONE
CHINA

FENTON
STONE WORKS

MEISSON
1713

1713-1724   1725-1750   modern

MENNECY
1734-1748

D V
incised

D.V.
in blue

MINTON
1793 onwards

1800-1836   1851   1860-1880

MINTON B B New Stone   MINTONS
1861 onward   20th century

NANTGARW
1811-1820

Nantgarw
1811

NANTGARW
1813

SWANSEA
NANGARW
1814

NANT GARW
C.W.
1816-1820

14

NEWHALL 1782-1835

PETIT JACOB 1796-1862

PLYMOUTH 1768-1772

ROCKINGHAM

early 19th century

SEVRES 1745

blue pre 1753

blue 1780

blue 1793-1804

red 1804-1814

blue 1814-1824

1824-1830

1834

1852-1870

SPODE 1770

1770-1797

impressed 1784

SPODE & COPELAND 1813

1813-1833

VIENNA 1719-1864

blue 1744-1820

blue 1750-1780

1850-1864

modern

WEDGWOOD 1730-1795

modern

WORCESTER

Dr. Wall 1751-1783

Flight 1783-1793

Flight & Barr 1793-1807

1807-1829

1850

1851

RECOGNITION & DATING - SOME USEFUL HINTS.

Obviously the task of committing every china mark to memory is one which will be outside the scope of most collectors and, indeed, most dealers too. For this reason, the following simple guides may prove to be of some assistance in determining the approximate date of a piece without having recourse to long, and frequently involved, lists of the marks used by various manufacturers over the years.

Any piece bearing the words 'English Bone China' or simply 'Bone China' is a product of the twentieth century and the words 'Made in England' also suggest twentieth century manufacture, though they could relate to pieces dating from 1875 onward.

The word 'England' stamped on a piece suggests compliance with the McKinley Tariff Act of America, 1891 which required all imports to America to bear the name of the country of origin.

In 1862, the Trade Mark Act became law. Any piece bearing the words 'Trade Mark' therefore, can be assumed to date from 1862 onward.

Following the law relating to companies of limited liability, the word Limited or its abbreviations appears after 1860, though more commonly on pieces dating from 1885 onwards.

When a piece bears a pattern number or name, it can be assumed to date no earlier than about 1810.

Royal Arms incorporated into a mark indicates a date after 1800.

During the mid 1800's, the word 'Royal' was commonly added to the Manufacturer's name or trade name and, consequently, pieces bearing this word can usually be placed after 1850.

HANDLES

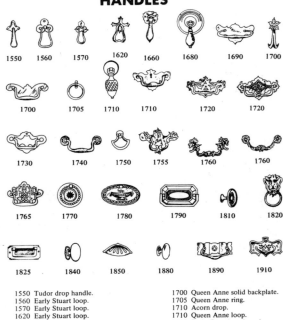

1550 Tudor drop handle.
1560 Early Stuart loop.
1570 Early Stuart loop.
1620 Early Stuart loop.
1660 Stuart drop.
1680 Stuart drop.
1690 William & Mary solid backplate.
1700 William & Mary split tail.

1750 Georgian shield drop.
1755 French style.
1760 French style.
1760 Rococo style.
1765 Chinese style.
1770 Georgian ring.
1780 Late Georgian stamped.
1790 Late Georgian stamped.

1700 Queen Anne solid backplate.
1705 Queen Anne ring.
1710 Acorn drop.
1710 Queen Anne loop.
1720 Early Georgian pierced.
1720 Early Georgian brass drop.
1730 Cut away backplate.
1740 Georgian plain brass loop.

1810 Regency knob.
1820 Regency lions mask.
1825 Campaign.
1840 Early Victorian porcelain.
1850 Victorian reeded.
1880 Porcelain or wood knob.
1890 Late Victorian loop.
1910 Art Nouveau.

PEDIMENTS

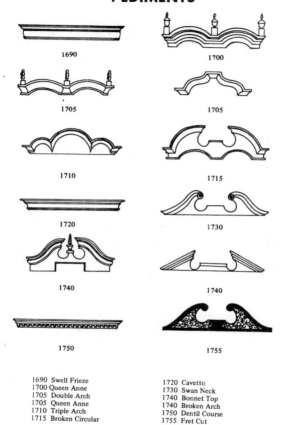

1690

1700

1705

1705

1710

1715

1720

1730

1740

1740

1750

1755

1690 Swell Frieze
1700 Queen Anne
1705 Double Arch
1705 Queen Anne
1710 Triple Arch
1715 Broken Circular

1720 Cavetto
1730 Swan Neck
1740 Bonnet Top
1740 Broken Arch
1750 Dentil Course
1755 Fret Cut

FEET

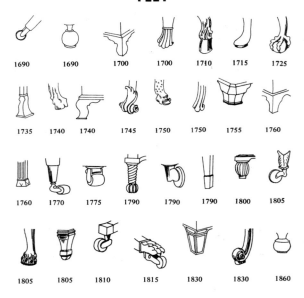

1690   1690   1700   1700   1710   1715   1725

1735   1740   1740   1745   1750   1750   1755   1760

1760   1770   1775   1790   1790   1790   1800   1805

1805   1805   1810   1815   1830   1830   1860

1690 Wooden Wheel	1760 Gutta Foot
1690 Ball.	1770 Tapered Socket
1700 Bracket	1775 Peg and Plate
1700 Spanish	1790 Spiral Twist
1710 Hoof	1790 Wheel Castor
1715 Pad	1790 Spade
1725 Ball and Claw	1800 Fluted Ball
1735 Cabriole Leg Foot	1805 Decorative Socket
1740 Stylised Hoof	1805 Paw
1740 Ogee	1805 Regency
1745 French Knurl	1810 Horizontal Socket
1750 Dolphin	1815 Lions Paw
1750 English Knurl	1830 Regency
1755 Elaborate Bracket	1830 Victorian Scroll
1760 Splay	1860 Victorian Bun

LEGS

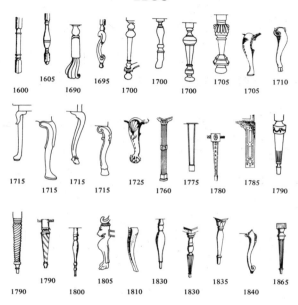

1600 Elizabethan Turned	1760 Cluster Column
1605 Stuart Baluster	1775 Square Tapering
1690 Spanish	1780 Sheraton Tapered
1695 William and Mary 'S' Curve	1785 Chinese Chippendale
1700 Trumpet	1790 Turned and Tapered
1700 Portuguese Bulb	1790 Tapered Scroll
1700 Mushroom	1790 Tapered Spiral
1705 Inverted Cup	1800 Windsor Turned
1705 Queen Anne Cabriole	1805 Lions Paw
1710 Hoof Foot	1810 Regency Sabre
1715 Modified Cabriole	1830 Windsor Baluster
1715 Pad Foot	1830 Turned and Fluted
1715 Cabriole	1835 Victorian Turned
1715 Hoof	1840 Victorian Cabriole
1725 Ball and Claw	1865 Victorian Reeded

19

CHAIR BACKS

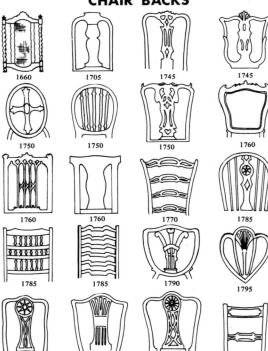

1660
1705
1745
1745
1750
1750
1750
1760
1760
1760
1770
1785
1785
1785
1790
1795
1795
1795
1795
1810

1660 Charles II
1705 Queen Anne
1745 Chippendale
1745 Chippendale
1750 Georgian
1750 Hepplewhite
1750 Chippendale
1760 French Rococo
1760 Gothic
1760 Splat Back

1770 Chippendale Ladder Back
1785 Windsor wheel back
1785 Lancashire Spindle Back
1785 Lancashire Ladder Back
1790 Shield and Feathers
1795 Shield Back
1795 Hepplewhite
1795 Hepplewhite Camel Back
1795 Hepplewhite
1810 Late Georgian Bar Back

CHAIR BACKS

1810

1810

1815

1815

1820

1820

1820

1825

1830

1830

1830

1830

1835

1840

1845

1845

1850

1860

1870

1875

1810 Thomas Hope 'X' Frame
1810 Regency Rope Back
1815 Regency.
1815 Regency Cane Back.
1820 Regency
1820 Empire
1820 Regency Bar Back
1825 Regency Bar Back
1830 Regency Bar Back
1830 Bar Back

1830 William IV Bar Back
1830 William IV
1835 Lath Back
1840 Victorian Balloon Back
1845 Victorian
1845 Victorian Bar Back
1850 Victorian
1860 Victorian
1870 Victorian
1875 Cane Back

BUREAUX

1

Dutch mahogany bombe front, cylinder desk with shaped interior.

2

Edwardian oak bureau on stretcher base.

3

18th century oak bureau with fluted pillars.

4

Georgian mahogany bureau on bracket feet.

5

Edwardian inlaid mahogany cylinder front bureau.

6

Edwardian inlaid mahogany bureau with cupboard under.

7

Edwardian Sheraton style bureau with cylinder top and cupboard under.

8

Small George III mahogany bureau on ogee feet.

9

Queen Anne walnut bureau on stand.

10

French mahogany bureau with inlaid flowers and ormolu mounts.

11

George II bureau in burr ash crossbanded with walnut.

12

Early 17th century oak bureau on bun feet.

22

1

Georgian mahogany bureau
on splayed feet.

2

Georgian satinwood desk
with tambour.

3

Late 19th century lacquered
bureau on cabriole legs.

4

Early 18th century oak
bureau with stand.

5

Sheraton style sandlewood
bureau.

6

Edwardian mahogany bureau
with shell inlay and bracket
feet.

7

French marquetry and rosewood bureau with brass
gallery and cabriole legs.

8

Edwardian inlaid mahogany
cylinder front bureau.

9

William and Mary walnut
bureau on stand.

10

Early Georgian mahogany
bureau on stand.

11

17th century oak desk on
turned leg supports with
stretchers.

12

Queen Anne bureau in walnut
with herringbone banding.

23

BUREAU BOOKCASES

1
Early 20th century oak bureau bookcase.

2
George I yew wood bureau bookcase with broken arched pediment.

3
Burr yew wood cylinder desk and bookcase with satinwood, kingwood and tulipwood enrichments.

4
Small Queen Anne bureau bookcase with the upper front having a moulded cornice.

5
Hepplewhite period bureau bookcase in mahogany with latticed glazed doors.

6
George II bureau bookcase with bevelled Vauxhall mirror door

7
Mid 18th century bureau bookcase in mahogany.

8
Mid 18th century bombe shaped Continental bureau bookcase in mahogany.

9
George II style red and gold lacquered bureau bookcase.

10
Late 18th century German mahogany bureau bookcase.

11
Late 18th century mahogany bureau bookcase with glazed doors in the Gothic manner.

12
Edwardian mahogany bureau bookcase on cabriole leg supports.

Queen Anne walnut
bureau bookcase with
a stepped interior.

Small Edwardian inlaid
bureau bookcase with
a single astragal glazed
door.

Victorian cylinder top
kneehole bureau bookcase
in mahogany, on bun feet.

Small Queen Anne
walnut bureau book-
case.

Early 18th century
Flemish marquetry
bureau cabinet.

George II mahogany
bureau cabinet on
ogee feet.

Edwardian Sheraton
style cylinder front
bureau bookcase
with glazed doors.

Edwardian oak bureau
bookcase with leaded
glazing.

Georgian mahogany
bureau bookcase with
astragal glazed doors.

George II walnut
bureau bookcase with
double domed top.

Edwardian inlaid
mahogany bureau
bookcase.

Small 18th century
Dutch marquetry
bureau cabinet.

25

BEDS

1

Victorian brass bed 3ft wide.

2

A Victorian brass childs bed.

3

A Victorian brass half tester bed 4ft6ins. wide.

4

Italian carved walnut four poster bed.

5

French mahogany bed with crisply carved cresting and rubbed gilt enrichments,circa 1860.

6

17th century oak four poster bed.

7

Regency mahogany bed with ormolu decoration and paw feet.

8

19th century Dutch marquetry bed 3ft., wide.

9

Regency mahogany bed inlaid with satinwood.

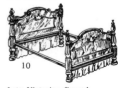

10

Late Victorian figured mahogany bed, 4ft.6ins., wide.

11

Early Georgian mahogany tester with original drapes. 4ft 6 ins., wide.

12

19th century red lacquer and gilt bed 4ft. wide, decorated with domestic scenes.

1

Early 19th century oak cot.

2

Victorian wicker work cradle.

3

Hepplewhite mahogany canework crib.

4

A Victorian brass crib.

5

A late 18th century mahogany crib.

6

A 17th century Continental oak crib.

7

19th century country made chair back crib in elm.

8

Late 17th century oak hooded cradle.

9

17th century oak cradle.

10

Sheraton period crib with a mechanical rocker.

11

A 17th century oak box cradle.

12

Late Georgian suspended cot in canework

BOOKCASES

1

A small French Empire bookcase with a marble top and brass gallery.

2

Edwardian mahogany revolving bookcase inlaid with bone and ivory.

3

Regency period open shelf brass inlaid bookcase in rosewood with marble top.

4

Victorian mahogany hanging shelves with small drawer in base.

5

Victorian mahogany open bookshelves.

6

Late Georgian satinwood bookcase.

7

Regency mahogany bookcase fitted with adjustable shelves and gilt tooled leather swags.

8

Regency period ebonised standing bookshelves

9

George III bookcase in finely grained mahogany.

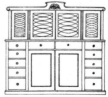

10

Georgian mahogany breakfront bookcase with glazed doors.

11

18th century mahogany breakfront bookcase

12

Regency mahogany library bookcase circa 1820.

1

19th century rosewood
open bookcase, circa 1835.

2

Small Regency mahogany
bookcase on stand with a
brass grille door.

3

Regency brass inlaid rosewood bookcase.

4

Victorian mahogany
standing bookcase.

5

Regency mahogany break-
front bookcase with brass
grille to cupboard doors.

6

Regency period mahogany
open bookshelves, circa 1820.

7

Regency period Gothic style
bookcase with glazed doors.

8

A late Victorian mahogany
bookcase with glazed doors.

9

Sheraton mahogany bookcase
with diamond shaped glazing
bars, circa 1790.

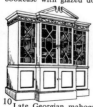

10 Late Georgian mahogany
breakfront bookcase.

11

George III mahogany breakfront bookcase with satinwood stringing.

12

Victorian breakfront
bookcase in mahogany.

29

DINING CHAIRS

1

Hepplewhite mahogany
dining chair, circa 1785.

2

Victorian mahogany
bar back chair on turned
legs.

3

A Windsor stick
back chair.

4

A Chippendale chair.

5

Victorian splat back
kitchen chair in elm.

6

Hepplewhite period
mahogany dining
chair.

7

Regency period mahogany
dining chair with scimitar
shaped legs.

8

Late 19th
century dining
chair

9

Charles II walnut
dining chair.

10

Victorian bentwood
dining chair.

11

Early Victorian
simulated rosewood
bedroom chair.

12

Queen Anne dining
chair veneered in
walnut.

13

Victorian oak Gothic
style dining chair.

14

19th century elm
kitchen chair.

15

Derbyshire oak dining
chair.

16

Mid 18th century
mahogany servants
hall chair.

30

1

Chippendale style
mahogany chair,
circa 1840.

2

Regency mahogany
dining chair with 'X'
frame back.

3

Early 19th century 4
mahogany dining
chair on turned legs.

Mid Victorian mahogany
dining chair.

5

French rococo
style dining
chair in giltwood.

6

A Regency chair with
drop in seat.

7

An early oak ladder back
chair with a rush seat.

8

William IV mahogany
frame dining chair.

9

Dutch marquetry
chair

10

Victorian cabriole
leg dining chair.

11

Hepplewhite style dining
chair in mahogany.

12

William III walnut
dining chair.

13

Regency mahogany
dining chair

14

Early Victorian
hall chair.

15

Early Victorian mahogany
balloon back dining chair.

16

Late Victorian oak
framed dining chair.

31

ELBOW CHAIRS

1

Late Georgian elbow chair.

Early Victorian mahogany elbow chair.

Mid 18th century mahogany corner chair.

William IV mahogany elbow chair on turned legs.

5

George I walnut veneered armchair.

19th century bentwood rocking chair.

Edwardian inlaid mahogany elbow chair.

Fine Hepplewhite period armchair.

9

Regency mahogany sabre leg carver.

Chippendale mahogany ladder back carving chair.

Lath and baluster back Windsor chair.

Hepplewhite shield back chair.

Charles II walnut high chair.

Late Georgian Windsor wheel back armchair.

Edwardian inlaid mahogany corner chair.

American desk chair in ash.

32

1
Regency period elbow chair with brass string inlay.

2
Regency 'X' back mahogany elbow chair on sabre legs.

3
William IV mahogany carver.

4
Queen Anne walnut armchair, circa 1710.

5
Regency period childs chair.

6
Windsor wheelback childs high chair in elm.

7
Queen Anne black japanned chair with caned seat and back.

8
Early George II walnut armchair.

9
Victorian papier mache salon chair.

10
Victorian smokers chair in elm.

11
William IV dining chair upholstered in brown hide.

12
Cromwellian armchair.

13
Regency period elbow chair.

14
Carved Jacobean oak hall chair.

15
Early 19th century childs high chair.

16
A Yorkshire ladder back.

33

EASY CHAIRS

1 19th century mahogany framed sewing chair.

2 Mid Victorian papier mache prie dieu chair

3 Edwardian mahogany occasional chair.

4 Victorian mahogany block arm grandfather chair.

5 Louis XV period giltwood Bergere, circa 1760.

6 Late Victorian horse-shoe backed chair.

7 Early Victorian rosewood framed gents armchair.

8 Louis XV giltwood arm-chair.

9 Late 18th century oval backed armchair.

10 Victorian iron frame ladies chair.

11 Victorian walnut prie dieu chair

12 18th century French armchair.

13 Victorian Abbotsford chair in walnut.

14 Victorian mahogany cabriole leg grand-father chair.

15 Hepplewhite period Gainsborough chair.

16 Edwardian ebonised horseshoe back chair.

34

1 Victorian balloon back ladies chair on cabriole leg supports.

2 Small Victorian buttoned sewing chair.

3 Mid 18th century library chair.

4 Edwardian inlaid walnut nursing chair.

5 Regency library chair.

6 Victorian nursing chair with a bead and needlework cover.

7 Late Victorian armchair.

8 Late Victorian ebonised occasional chair.

9 George II mahogany armchair on cluster column legs.

10 Victorian prie dieu chair supported on turned legs.

11 Victorian walnut frame horseshoe back smokers chair.

12 Chippendale period mahogany armchair.

13 A 17th century English panelled oak chair.

14 Late 18th century wing chair.

15 Late 19th century easy chair.

16 Regency period giltwood chair.

35

COUCHES

1 Georgian mahogany settee on cabriole legs.

2 An unusual Gothic style sofa and steps, circa 1820.

3 Edwardian ebonised settee on tapered legs.

4 Small Regency period settee in rosewood with brass mounts and brass claw feet.

5 Victorian heavily upholstered drop end couch.

6 Victorian sofa in walnut on cabriole legs.

7 Hepplewhite period settee on tapered legs.

8 Early Victorian cabriole leg couch.

9 Victorian ottoman supported on cabriole legs.

10 A Louis XV carved giltwood settee on cabriole legs.

11 Edwardian inlaid mahogany Sheraton style settee.

12 Victorian two seater Chesterfield.

13 Victorian single end chaise longue.

14 Early carved oak hall seat in elm.

15 19th century gilded day bed.

36

1 Edwardian inlaid mahogany settee on square tapering legs.

2 18th century Gothic style mahogany couch.

3 17th century oak settee.

5 Victorian couch with carved mahogany frame on turned legs.

4 Victorian scroll end mahogany sofa on turned legs.

6 Regency period scroll end sofa.

8 Mid 18th century Continental giltwood triple back settee.

7 Victorian mahogany framed sofa.

9 William IV mahogany salon sofa.

10 A 19th century love seat.

11 19th century kidney shape settee.

12 Louis XV giltwood settee on carved cabriole legs.

13 18th century settee on cabriole legs with ball and claw feet.

14 Victorian papier mache sofa inlaid with mother of pearl.

15 Hepplewhite period mahogany settee.

CHESTS

1

A Dutch oak bombe front chest.

2

Victorian Wellington chest veneered in rosewood.

3

Queen Anne bachelors chest in walnut .

4

19th century Dutch marquetry chest of drawers.

5

A Dutch marquetry bombe chest of drawers decorated with tulips and sycamore leaves.

6

Late Georgian serpentine front mahogany chest.

7

A William and Mary walnut chest on stand with bun feet.

8

William and Mary oyster veneered laburnum chest of drawers with boxwood stringing.

9

A Queen Anne walnut bachelors chest, circa 1710.

10

Period oak chest of drawers on bun feet.

11

An early 18th century oyster veneered walnut chest of drawers.

12

Victorian mahogany chest of drawers.

1
Georgian mahogany chest of drawers on ogee feet.

2
A serpentine front chest of four drawers in coromandel wood, circa 1800.

3
A William and Mary walnut chest of drawers.

4
An early 18th century walnut chest of drawers with canted corners.

5
Sheraton satinwood bow fronted chest, crossbanded in tulipwood with ebony and boxwood stringing.

6
A Chippendale mahogany chest of drawers having quartered columns, circa 1760.

7
Victorian stripped pine chest of drawers on turned feet.

8
A George I chest in finely figured mahogany with brass carrying handles.

9
Regency mahogany shaped front chest of drawers.

10
An 18th century block front chest of drawers.

11
18th century mahogany chest with a brushing slide.

12

Georgian mahogany bow front chest with boxwood lines.

39

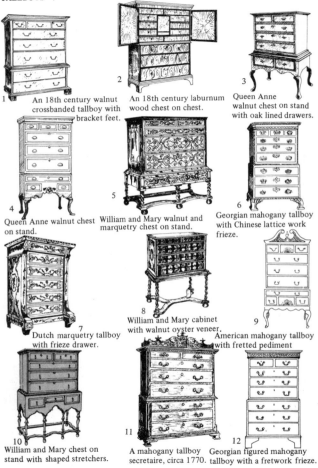

1   An 18th century walnut crossbanded tallboy with bracket feet.

2   An 18th century laburnum wood chest on chest.

3   Queen Anne walnut chest on stand with oak lined drawers.

4   Queen Anne walnut chest on stand.

5   William and Mary walnut and marquetry chest on stand.

6   Georgian mahogany tallboy with Chinese lattice work frieze.

7   Dutch marquetry tallboy with frieze drawer.

8   William and Mary cabinet with walnut oyster veneer.

9   American mahogany tallboy with fretted pediment

10   William and Mary chest on stand with shaped stretchers.

11   A mahogany tallboy secretaire, circa 1770.

12   Georgian figured mahogany tallboy with a fretwork frieze.

1

George I crossbanded walnut tallboy having a Norwich Sunburst decoration.

2

A walnut chest of drawers on stand, circa 1770.

3

A mahogany bow front chest on chest with a dentil cornice.

4

A Georgian mahogany tallboy, circa 1820.

5

A William and Mary chest on stand with oyster veneers on twist supports with shaped stretchers.

6

18th century walnut tallboy with fluted pilasters to the top section.

7

American fruitwood highboy on cabriole legs.

8

William and Mary burr elm and walnut chest on stand.

9

George III mahogany tallboy.

10

Victorian mahogany tallboy on splay feet.

11

A Queen Anne banded mulberry wood chest on stand.

12

18th century mahogany tallboy with brass capitals.

41

COMMODE CHESTS

1

Late 18th century two door commode in the manner of John Cobb.

2

Late Georgian semi circular commode in satinwood inlaid with bows and ribbons.

3

17th century commode in walnut and holly.

4

Georgian shaped front inlaid satinwood commode.

5

18th century Dutch mahogany bombe shaped commode. 6

A serpentine front Continental commode with two drawers and a marble top.

7

Dutch marquetry walnut commode with bombe front and sides.

8

A small Louis XV style marquetry commode on cabriole shaped supports.

9

18th century inlaid bombe shape commode with grey marble top.

11

10

Georgian serpentine front commode in mellow mahogany.

Small Italian walnut commode inlaid with satinwood.

12

18th century French Provencal double serpentine front commode in walnut.

42

French commode in kingwood and tulipwood with rose marble top and ormolu decoration.

19th century French commode inlaid with floral marquetry.

Georgian serpentine front commode in satinwood decorated with musical instruments and ribbons.

19th century kingwood marquetry and parquetry commode.

Louis XV petite commode in kingwood and rosewood with ormolu mounts.

An 18th century Dutch marquetry and rosewood crossbanded straight front commode.

Louis XV marquetry and kingwood commode with a marble top.

Small French marquetry commode.

18th century Dutch marquetry commode in yew wood.

18th century serpentine shaped commode inlaid with various woods and with a rouge marble top.

A Dutch 18th century commode in rosewood.

Hepplewhite shaped front commode in satinwood.

CANTERBURYS

1
Victorian rosewood canterbury with drawer to base.

2
An early Victorian papier mache canterbury decorated with mother of pearl and gilt.

3
Regency mahogany canterbury on fine turned legs.

4
Unusual Georgian mahogany canterbury with drawer to base.

5
Small Victorian burr walnut canterbury.

6
A rosewood music canterbury with lyre motifs, circa 1820.

7
Georgian mahogany canterbury on fine turned feet.

8
Victorian burr walnut music canterbury with fretted supports.

9
Late Georgian mahogany canterbury.

10
An early Victorian burr walnut music canterbury.

11
A Regency period rosewood canterbury.

12
Regency mahogany canterbury with drawer.

13
Regency mahogany canterbury on short turned legs.

14
A Victorian ebonised canterbury on bun feet.

15
William IV mahogany music canterbury.

44

Georgian mahogany commode.

Late Georgian mahogany commode with lift up top.

Regency night commode in figured mahogany.

A Victorian cylindrical mahogany pot cupboard.

Victorian three step commode.

Victorian mahogany pot cupboard with a marble top.

Victorian commode in walnut.

A Victorian mahogany commode.

Small Victorian mahogany one step commode.

Regency bedroom cupboard.

An early Georgian mahogany pot cupboard.

Georgian mahogany tray top commode.

Chippendale mahogany pot cupboard.

Late Georgian mahogany tray top commode.

Georgian tray top night table in satinwood.

45

CORNER CABINETS

1
An early 18th century yew wood corner cabinet with a glazed door and shaped shelves.

2
Mahogany corner cupboard with shaped shelves, circa 1800.

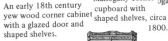

Georgian bow front mahogany corner cupboard

3

4
Early 18th century black japanned corner cupboard.

5
Queen Anne walnut standing corner cupboard.

6
Late Georgian mahogany diamond glazed corner cupboard with satinwood inlay.

7
Late Georgian mahogany corner cupboard on ogee feet.

8
Georgian mahogany corner cupboard with astragal glazed doors.

9
18th century oak dole cupboard with centre drawer and four shelves.

10
Sheraton period mahogany corner cupboard with satinwood inlay.

11
A Georgian oak corner cupboard with a centre drawer and panelled doors.

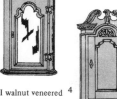

2

Late Georgian mahogany corner cupboard.

1

Early 18th century corner cupboard.

George I walnut veneered corner cupboard with mirrored doors.

4

Late Georgian walnut veneered corner cupboard.

5

Georgian mahogany corner cupboard with astragal glazed doors.

Late Georgian finely grained mahogany bow fronted corner cupboard.

7

An 18th century oak corner cupboard with panelled doors and bracket feet.

8

Edwardian inlaid mahogany corner cupboard.

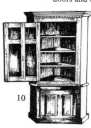

9

George II bow fronted corner cupboard in mahogany.

10

A stripped pine corner cupboard with a panelled cupboard door enclosing three shelves, circa 1740.

11

Georgian stripped pine corner cupboard.

CHINA CABINETS

1

An early Victorian burr walnut display cabinet.

2

19th century marquetry specimen table.

3

Late 19th century ebonised display cabinet.

4

Georgian ebonised display cabinet.

5

A Louis Phillipe corner display shelf.

6

Small Edwardian inlaid mahogany specimen cabinet.

7

Victorian walnut music cabinet.

8

Late Georgian mahogany display cabinet.

9

Chinese style Georgian mahogany display cabinet.

10

19th century Chinese hardwood display cabinet.

11

Early 19th century French display cabinet.

12

19th century French display cabinet.

13

Edwardian inlaid mahogany china cabinet.

14

19th century French cabinet in kingwood.

15

French cabinet, circa 1860.

48

1

19th century black and red boulle display cabinet.

2

Edwardian inlaid mahogany specimen table on tapered legs.

3

18th century Sheraton inlaid satinwood hanging display cabinet.

4

Small Edwardian inlaid mahogany display cabinet.

5

Late 19th century inlaid mahogany specimen cabinet.

6

Edwardian inlaid kidney shaped specimen table.

7

A French Empire bijouterie.

8

A Chippendale period display cabinet.

9

Louis Phillipe cabinet with Vernis Martin panels.

10

French walnut display cabinet inlaid with ebony.

11

Edwardian corner cabinet.

12

19th century Venetian walnut display cabinet.

13

19th century gilt display cabinet

14

Edwardian inlaid mahogany china cabinet.

15

19th century kingwood vitrine.

49

CHIFFONIERS and CREDENZAS

1
A Regency period japanned chiffonier, circa 1810

2
Regency mahogany buffet.

3
Regency mahogany chiffonier.

4
Regency cabinet in rosewood.

5
Regency chiffonier in rosewood.

6
Regency mahogany cabinet.

7
Regency rosewood chiffonier with brass grilles to the doors.

8
Victorian mahogany chiffonier.

9
Early Victorian rosewood chiffonier.

10
Victorian burr walnut credenza.

11
Late Victorian walnut dressing table.

12
An early Victorian breakfront credenza.

13
Louis XVI credenza.

14
Early 19th century breakfront chiffonier.

15
19th century burr walnut and kingwood credenza.

1

Regency brass inlaid
rosewood chiffonier.

2

Small Regency brass
inlaid chiffonier.

3

Georgian chiffonier
in satinwood.

4

Late Victorian chiffonier

5

Regency mahogany bookcase
crossbanded in satinwood.

6

Victorian figured
mahogany chiffonier.

Victorian mahogany
chiffonier.

7

Regency chiffonier
in rosewood with
paw feet.

8

9

Regency mahogany
chiffonier with a
figured marble top.

10

Early 19th century gilt
credenza.

11

An early Victorian burr
walnut sideboard

12

An early 19th century boulle credenza.

13

Victorian chiffonier

14

An Italian gilt credenza with
a shaped marble top.

15

A mid Victorian ebonised cabinet.

DAVENPORTS

1

Regency mahogany sliding top davenport with four drawers.

2

Small Regency period davenport with oak lined drawers.

3

Regency rosewood davenport with a sliding top and scroll feet.

4

A simulated coromandel wood davenport of the Regency period.

5

George III mahogany sliding top davenport on bracket feet.

6

Edwardian red mahogany davenport with cupboard enclosing four drawers.

7

Victorian walnut davenport.

8

Edwardian inlaid mahogany davenport on tapered legs with cross stretchers.

9

Victorian burr walnut piano top davenport with rising top.

10

Chinese Chippendale style mahogany davenport.

11

Early Victorian piano top burr walnut davenport with a pull out adjustable writing slide.

12

Edwardian inlaid mahogany davenport with cupboard under.

Victorian cylindrical davenport in burr walnut.

Regency ladies writing table in mahogany.

Victorian davenport veneered in burr walnut.

William IV mahogany davenport.

Victorian inlaid walnut davenport on twist supports with two shelves under.

Regency period rosewood davenport on fluted legs.

An early Victorian davenport with turned and fluted front supports.

19th century teak military desk and stand.

A Victorian walnut davenport with a pull out pen and ink tray.

Victorian burr walnut davenport with cabriole leg front supports.

William IV mahogany davenport with pillar supports.

Victorian burr walnut serpentine fronted davenport.

DRESSERS

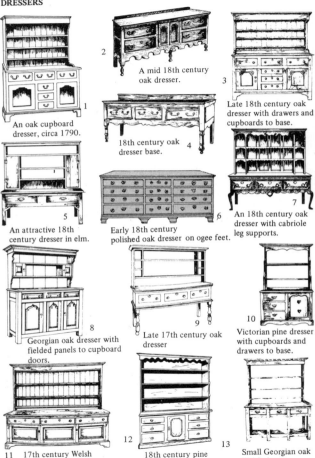

An oak cupboard dresser, circa 1790. **1**

A mid 18th century oak dresser. **2**

Late 18th century oak dresser with drawers and cupboards to base. **3**

18th century oak dresser base. **4**

An attractive 18th century dresser in elm. **5**

Early 18th century polished oak dresser on ogee feet. **6**

An 18th century oak dresser with cabriole leg supports. **7**

Georgian oak dresser with fielded panels to cupboard doors. **8**

Late 17th century oak dresser **9**

Victorian pine dresser with cupboards and drawers to base. **10**

17th century Welsh dresser in oak **11**

18th century pine farmhouse dresser **12**

Small Georgian oak Welsh dresser. **13**

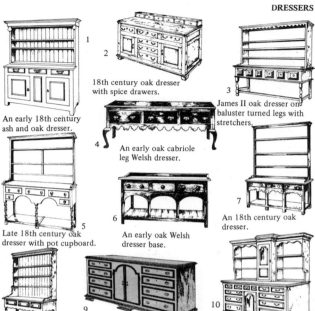

An early 18th century ash and oak dresser.

18th century oak dresser with spice drawers.

James II oak dresser on baluster turned legs with stretchers.

An early oak cabriole leg Welsh dresser.

Late 18th century oak dresser with pot cupboard.

An early oak Welsh dresser base.

An 18th century oak dresser.

Late Georgian oak dresser with bobbin turned legs

Late 18th century Lancashire dresser

George II Lancashire oak dresser.

Unusually small Georgian oak dresser with pot board.

Early Georgian oak dresser with pot board.

An unusual Welsh dresser, circa 1770.

DRESSING TABLES

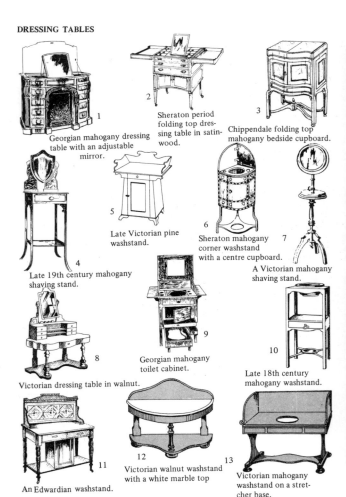

Georgian mahogany dressing table with an adjustable mirror. 1

Sheraton period folding top dressing table in satinwood. 2

Chippendale folding top mahogany bedside cupboard. 3

Late 19th century mahogany shaving stand. 4

Late Victorian pine washstand. 5

Sheraton mahogany corner washstand with a centre cupboard. 6

A Victorian mahogany shaving stand. 7

Victorian dressing table in walnut. 8

Georgian mahogany toilet cabinet. 9

Late 18th century mahogany washstand. 10

An Edwardian washstand. 11

Victorian walnut washstand with a white marble top 12

Victorian mahogany washstand on a stretcher base. 13

1

A Queen Anne walnut escritoire on bracket feet.

2

19th century amboyna wood escritoire on stand with a writing slide.

William and Mary secretaire cabinet.

4

William and Mary period walnut escritoire

5

Early 19th century secretaire a abattant

6

William and Mary figured walnut escritoire on stand.

7

Dutch marquetry escritoire

8

French escritoire with Sevres plaques and ormolu mounts.

9

17th century walnut writing cabinet.

Late 18th century French secretaire cabinet veneered with kingwood.

11

Victorian mahogany escritoire on bun feet.

12

French Empire ladies escritoire in mahogany.

13

18th century laburnum wood chest on chest.

57

LOWBOYS

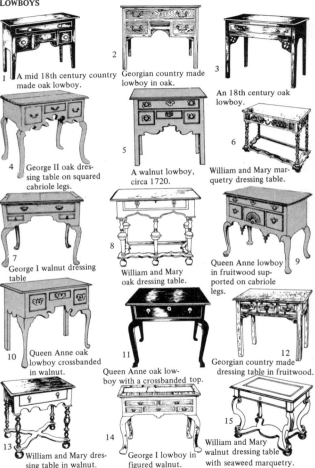

1 A mid 18th century country made oak lowboy.

2 Georgian country made lowboy in oak.

3 An 18th century oak lowboy.

4 George II oak dressing table on squared cabriole legs.

5 A walnut lowboy, circa 1720.

6 William and Mary marquetry dressing table.

7 George I walnut dressing table

8 William and Mary oak dressing table.

9 Queen Anne lowboy in fruitwood supported on cabriole legs.

10 Queen Anne oak lowboy crossbanded in walnut.

11 Queen Anne oak lowboy with a crossbanded top.

12 Georgian country made dressing table in fruitwood.

13 William and Mary dressing table in walnut.

14 George I lowboy in figured walnut.

15 William and Mary walnut dressing table with seaweed marquetry.

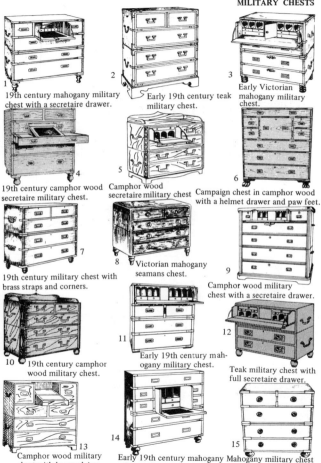

1 19th century mahogany military chest with a secretaire drawer.

2 Early 19th century teak military chest.

3 Early Victorian mahogany military chest.

4 19th century camphor wood secretaire military chest.

5 Camphor wood secretaire military chest

6 Campaign chest in camphor wood with a helmet drawer and paw feet.

7 19th century military chest with brass straps and corners.

8 Victorian mahogany seamans chest.

9 Camphor wood military chest with a secretaire drawer.

10 19th century camphor wood military chest.

11 Early 19th century mahogany military chest.

12 Teak military chest with full secretaire drawer.

13 Camphor wood military chest with brass edging.

14 Early 19th century mahogany military chest.

15 Mahogany military chest with sunken handles.

59

PEDESTAL DESKS

1
Georgian mahogany kneehole desk on ogee feet.

2
George I walnut kneehole desk with recessed cupboard.

3
Victorian oak pedestal desk.

4
Late Georgian satinwood kneehole desk.

5
Writing desk formerly owned by Sir William Carr.

6
William and Mary walnut kneehole desk.

7
George II mahogany partners desk.

8
Late 19th century inlaid mahogany kneehole desk.

9
Chippendale period mahogany serpentine front kneehole desk.

10
Chippendale mahogany kneehole desk on ogee feet.

11
George III kneehole desk, circa 1790.

12
Early George III mahogany kneehole writing desk.

13
Regency period ebonised desk with brass moulding.

14
Early George III mahogany kneehole desk.

15
Regency period padouk wood pedestal desk.

1
Chippendale mahogany
writing desk.

2
19th century kidney shaped
burr walnut desk.

3
Victorian mahogany
pedestal desk.

4
Sheraton mahogany
kneehole desk.

5
Military style camphor
wood pedestal desk.

6
Late Georgian inlaid
mahogany kneehole desk.

7
Queen Anne kneehole desk
in walnut.

8
19th century boulle knee-
hole writing desk.

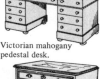

9
19th century mahogany
pedestal desk.

10
Georgian mahogany pedestal
desk enclosed by a tambour
shutter.

11
Late Victorian oak
pedestal desk.

12
Small 18th century
kneehole writing desk.

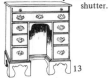

13
18th century mahogany
kneehole desk.

14
George I walnut
kneehole desk.

15
Victorian mahogany pedestal
desk with a cylinder top.

61

SECRETAIRES

1

Regency period chiffonier with fitted secretaire drawer.

2

Regency period Wellington chest with secretaire drawer.

3

19th century brass banded mahogany secretaire.

4

Georgian mahogany serpentine front secretaire chest.

5

George II mahogany bachelors chest, circa 1750.

Regency bonheur de jour in figured mahogany.

6

7

Hepplewhite secretaire bookcase.

8

Georgian mahogany secretaire bookcase.

9

George I burr yew wood domed top secretaire bookcase.

10

An early 18th century walnut secretaire tallboy.

11 Chippendale mahogany secretaire

12

Early 19th century secretaire bookcase.

13

Georgian mahogany secretaire

14

Hepplewhite secretaire bookcase.

1
Hepplewhite secretaire
chest in mahogany on
splay feet.

2
Late 18th century inlaid
mahogany secretaire.

Sheraton mahogany bow
fronted secretaire.

4
Late Victorian mahogany
secretaire chest on bun
feet.

5
George III mahogany
secretaire chest.

6
Chippendale figured mah-
ogany secretaire.

7
William IV mahogany
secretaire bookcase.

8
Regency mahogany
secretaire bookcase
veneered in zebra
wood.

9
Late 18th century
secretaire bookcase.

10
Georgian tallboy in mah-
ogany with secretaire
drawer.

11
Secretaire bookcase
in satinwood

12
18th century serpentine
front walnut writing
cabinet.

13
Chippendale mahogany
secretaire bookcase.

14
Chippendale
secretaire tallboy.

63

Late Victorian mahogany suite.

Edwardian inlaid mahogany suite.

Louis XV giltwood drawing room suite.

Small Victorian three piece suite.

Early Victorian three piece suite.

1

Victorian revolving
piano stool in rose-
wood on paw feet.

2

Regency period revol-
ving piano stool.

3

Victorian revolving piano
stool in papier mache.

4

Victorian mahogany rev-
olving piano stool on
platform base.

5

Georgian stool with
cluster column legs.

6

Regency 'X' frame
stool with cane seat.

7

Hepplewhite mahogany
window seat.

8

Victorian walnut
footstool on bun
feet.

9

Regency period foot-
stool in rosewood.

10

Victorian footstool with
a beadwork cover.

11

Victorian mahogany
footstool.

12

Early Victorian cab-
riole leg stool.

13

Tudor period oak joined
stool.

14

Regency period carved
giltwood stool.

15

Hepplewhite mahogany
stool on reeded legs.

16

Elizabethan style
foot stool.

17

Georgian mahogany
simulated bamboo
stool.

18

William and Mary foot-
stool in walnut.

TABLES

Regency mahogany dumb waiter. 1

Victorian lacquered table inlaid with ivory. 2

Victorian walnut Gypsy table. 3

Regency mahogany bedside table. 4

19th century red boulle occasional table. 5

Louis XV consol table. 6

Victorian mahogany cutlery stand. 7

Victorian occasional table in rosewood. 8

George III inlaid mahogany table. 9

Victorian inlaid burr walnut tripod table. 10

Late 18th century drum table. 11

Victorian games table. 12

Victorian mahogany bedside table. 13

Late Georgian architects table. 14

18th century tripod table. 15

18th century centre table. 16

Regency period reading desk. 17

Syrian hardwood table. 18

66

1 18th century elm cricket table.

2 Edwardian dark mahogany occasional table.

3 Victorian bamboo pot stand.

4 Louis Phillipe etagere

5 Charles II folding table in oak.

6 Sheraton period nest of tables.

7 A Georgian butler's tray.

8 19th century French table.

9 Early Victorian chess table.

10 Early 19th century gilded table.

11 19th century Japanese lacquer table.

12 Regency period stretcher table.

13 Regency period par-quetry top table.

14 Chinese Chippendale serving table.

15 Victorian mahogany occasional table.

16 A mahogany three tier dumb waiter, circa 1770.

17 Georgian mahogany snap top table.

18 Victorian papier mache tip top table.

TABLES

Regency mahogany card table.

Early Georgian
mahogany card table.

Victorian mahogany card table.

Victorian ebonised card table.

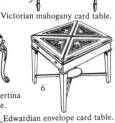
Georgian concertina
action tea table.

Edwardian envelope card table.

Queen Anne folding top
walnut card table.

19th century boulle card table.

Georgian satinwood card table.

Regency rosewood card table
with brass inlaid decoration.

Queen Anne folding table
inlaid with flowers.

Early Victorian rose-
wood card table.

Victorian inlaid burr
walnut card table.

Chinese Chippendale fold
over tea table.

Regency rosewood card table
crossbanded in satinwood.

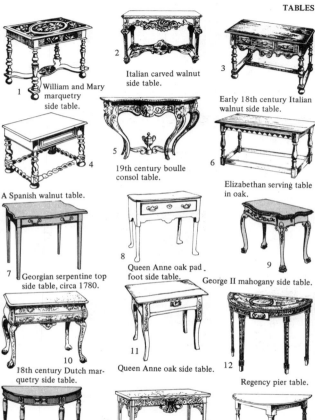

1 William and Mary marquetry side table.

2 Italian carved walnut side table.

3 Early 18th century Italian walnut side table.

4 A Spanish walnut table.

5 19th century boulle consol table.

6 Elizabethan serving table in oak.

7 Georgian serpentine top side table, circa 1780.

8 Queen Anne oak pad foot side table.

9 George II mahogany side table.

10 18th century Dutch marquetry side table.

11 Queen Anne oak side table.

12 Regency pier table.

13 Robert Adam giltwood side table.

14 Georgian side table with a marble top.

15 Cromwellian oak side table.

TABLES

1
Regency rosewood sofa table on stretcher base.

2
Late Sheraton sofa table in figured mahogany.

3
Regency rosewood sofa table crossbanded with satinwood.

4
Regency brass inlaid pedestal sofa table.

5
Brass inlaid Regency sofa table in rosewood.

6
Regency sofa table in rosewood on reeded legs.

7
Sheraton Pembroke table in satinwood.

8
Regency rosewood supper table with a crossbanded top.

9
Regency pedestal sofa table in mahogany.

10
17th century oak table with flap.

11
Late 18th century Irish wakes table.

12
A Victorian mahogany supper table.

13
Victorian Sutherland table.

14
Edwardian Sutherland table.

15
George III mahogany spider table.

70

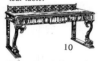

1

A Sheraton satinwood Pembroke table with butterfly wing leaves.

A late 18th century mahogany Pembroke table.

Early 19th century Pembroke table.

Georgian drop leaf cottage dining table.

Victorian stripped pine Pembroke table.

Regency mahogany concertina action dining table.

Chippendale mahogany drop leaf table.

Queen Anne oak gateleg table.

17th century oak gateleg table.

Regency period consol table, circa 1815.

Georgian envelope table.

Louis XV gilded wood consol table.

18th century rococo style consol table.

Small giltwood consol table, circa 1750.

Georgian consol table, circa 1740.

1
Regency rosewood
centre table.

2
Elizabeth I oak refectory table
with ground level stretchers.

3
Regency crossbanded
breakfast table.

4
An American extension
dining table, circa 1810.

5
George III dining table.

6
17th century oak drawleaf
table.

7
George III coromandel
wood library table.

8
Victorian marquetry
loo table.

9
Georgian triple pillar dining table.

10
Regency circular drum table.

11
Victorian walnut loo table.

12
19th century kingwood table.

13
Victorian centre table.

14
Victorian snap top table.

15
George III sectional dining table.

16
Victorian walnut table.

1 Georgian supper table.

2 17th century Spanish walnut table.

3 Regency centre table.

4 Large Regency mahogany table.

5 Late Victorian loo table.

6 George II table.

7 18th century mahogany drum table.

8 Thomas Hope Regency table.

9 Georgian oak refectory table.

10 Regency rosewood centre table.

11 Victorian oak hall table.

12 Georgian pillar dining table.

13 Victorian mahogany centre table.

14 Victorian loo table.

15 Victorian telescopic table.

16 Regency drum table.

73

SIDEBOARDS

1

Victorian carved oak sideboard.

2

Mid Victorian mahogany pedestal sideboard.

3

Early Victorian mahogany pedestal sideboard inlaid with ebony.

4

Georgian mahogany sideboard.

6

Regency sideboard in mahogany on fluted legs.

5

Edwardian red mahogany sideboard.

7

Georgian mahogany sideboard.

9

Late 18th century mahogany serpentine front sideboard.

8

A large Sheraton mahogany sideboard.

10

Sheraton mahogany breakfront sideboard.

13

Sheraton mahogany demi lune sideboard, circa 1790.

11

Georgian mahogany sideboard.

14

George III mahogany sideboard.

12

Regency period maple and satinwood sideboard.

Early Victorian mahogany pedestal sideboard.

Late Victorian rosewood sideboard inlaid with bone and ivory.

Regency period mahogany sideboard on paw feet.

Sheraton mahogany sideboard, circa 1780.

Sheraton period serpentine fronted sideboard.

Adam period mahogany sideboard on fine turned legs.

Edwardian mahogany sideboard.

Georgian mahogany sideboard.

Late Georgian concave front mahogany sideboard.

Late Victorian carved walnut sideboard.

Early 19th century inverted breakfront sideboard.

Late Georgian mahogany sideboard with a tambour front cupboard.

17th century oak sideboard.

Regency period mahogany sideboard on fine turned legs.

75

TRUNKS

Late 17th century oak chest.

17th century oak box on stand.

Oak coffer of plank construction, circa 1600

Mahogany bridal chest, circa 1780.

Jacobean oak food hutch, circa 1680.

An early 16th century Gothic style oak coffer.

Early 18th century leather and sealskin travelling box.

16th century Italian cassone in carved walnut.

18th century walnut chest decorated with herring bone inlay.

A William and Mary studded and decorated leather trunk.

Victorian mahogany sarcophagus shaped cellarette.

19th century brass bound camphor wood trunk.

17th century iron treasure chest.

Late 18th century Continental chest.

1

Georgian mahogany silver chest.

2

17th century oak bible box.

3

17th century oak mule chest.

4

17th century beechwood bread trough.

5

18th century elm dough bin on square legs with stretchers.

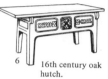

6

16th century oak hutch.

7

18th century Spanish carved walnut coffer.

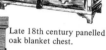

8

Late 18th century panelled oak blanket chest.

9

Late 18th century elm dower chest.

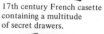

10

19th century German ebonised cabinet.

11

17th century French casette containing a multitude of secret drawers.

12

19th century brass bound mahogany box.

13

William and Mary period lacquered chest on stand.

14

Mid 16th century Riven oak chest.

WRITING TABLES

1 Edwardian inlaid mahogany writing table.

2 19th century boulle writing cabinet.

3 Louis XVI giltwood writing table.

4 A Victorian mahogany library table.

5 A Regency rosewood library table.

6 Regency mahogany writing table with drawers to both sides.

7 George III marquetry writing table.

8 French rosewood writing table.

9 Early Victorian mahogany library table.

10 George III table with fitted drawer.

11 Edwardian satinwood decorated writing table.

12 Empire style mahogany bureau a cylindre.

13 Mid Victorian bamboo writing table.

14 Edwardian writing table.

1
A Victorian ebonised
bonheur de jour.

2
Chippendale architects
table.

3
19th century rosewood
kidney shaped writing table.

4
Victorian rosewood library
table on a stretcher base.

5
Georgian mahogany
Carlton House writing
table.

7
Georgian Pembroke
writing table.

6
Victorian mahogany
writing table with car-
ved cabriole legs.

8
Edwardian mahogany
table desk.

9
Regency games table
in rosewood.

10
French walnut desk on
cabriole legs with ormolu
mounts and Sevres panels.

11
Edwardian writing desk.

12
19th century bureau
plat in kingwood.

13
Sheraton period mahogany
bonheur de jour.

14
18th century tambour
desk.

79

WORK BOXES

1

Victorian mahogany folding top work table.

2

Victorian burr walnut octagonal work box on carved cabriole legs.

3

Regency work table on tripod base.

4

19th century Tunbridge ware work table.

5

Sheraton workbox in harewood.

6

Sheraton period mahogany sewing table.

7

Regency work table in satinwood.

8

19th century French work table.

9

18th century mahogany sewing table.

10

Edwardian inlaid mahogany sewing table.

11

Early Victorian rose wood teapoy.

12

Regency work table in figured mahogany.

13

Late Regency rosewood teapoy inlaid with mother of pearl.

14

Mid Victorian black lacquered workbox.

15

Tunbridge ware workbox on splay feet.

16

Regency rosewood worktable.

1. Victorian burr walnut workbox.

2. Victorian teapoy in pollard oak on twist column supports.

3. A mid Victorian burr walnut work table.

4. Victorian walnut workbox with a chess board top.

5. Marquetry work table on turned legs.

6. A mid Victorian combined games and sewing table.

7. Victorian work table in mahogany on a centre column with platform base.

8. Regency period mahogany work table.

9. Early Victorian sewing table.

10. Sheraton mahogany sewing table crossbanded in partridgewood.

11. Regency mahogany work table on turned column supports and stretcher base.

12. Empire period mahogany work table.

13. Victorian burr walnut work table with a chess board top.

14. Regency figured mahogany work table supported on carved splay feet.

15. Regency period brass inlaid rosewood teapoy.

16. A Regency reading and sewing table.

81

WINE COOLERS

Sheraton mahogany wine cooler

Hepplewhite oval cellarette in mahogany

A George III banded and brass bound mahogany oval cellarette.

Early 19th century mahogany wine cooler.

George III mahogany cellarette on stand with brass carrying handles.

Mid 18th century mahogany wine waiter.

Georgian mahogany octagonal brass bound wine cooler.

19th century marquetry wine cooler.

Sheraton mahogany cellarette on turned leg supports.

George III mahogany brass bound wine cooler.

Georgian mahogany wine cooler, circa 1780.

Sheraton period figured mahogany wine cooler inlaid with satinwood.

Regency period mah
ogany whatnot.

William IV rosewood
whatnot with twist
supports.

Georgian mahogany
whatnot.

Late Georgian two tier
whatnot in mahogany.

Victorian inlaid wal-
nut corner whatnot.

Regency four tier what-
not in mahogany.

Regency whatnot in
rosewood.

Mid Victorian walnut
veneered whatnot.

Mid Victorian burr
walnut whatnot.

Victorian inlaid wal-
nut three tier what-
not.

Early Victorian burr
walnut whatnot.

19th century
marquetry etagere.

Sheraton
mahogany whatnot
with two drawers.

Early Victorian mah-
ogany whatnot.

WARDROBES AND CUPBOARDS

1

An Italian walnut cupboard, circa 1600.

2

17th century oak cupboard.

3

Victorian stripped pine wardrobe.

4

Early 17th century French cupboard in oak.

5

Mid 17th century oak livery cupboard.

6

Late Georgian mahogany clothes press.

7

Georgian oak cupboard with four drawers to the lower section.

8

Mid 18th century Continental wardrobe.

9

George II mahogany cupboard on carved cabriole legs.

10

Late Georgian mahogany wardrobe.

11

Elizabethan oak court cupboard.

12

Sheraton mahogany linen press.

84

1

Late Georgian mahogany hanging wardrobe.

2

Early 18th century oak cupboard.

3

18th century Dutch marquetry wardrobe.

4

Early 18th century oak clothes press.

5

16th century German oak sacristy cupboard.

6

Georgian oak collectors cabinet with key pattern frieze.

7

18th century French Provencal carved oak armoire.

8

17th century oak livery cupboard with panelled doors.

9

Small William IV mahogany cabinet.

10

Late 18th century mahogany wardrobe.

11

Late Georgian mahogany breakfront wardrobe.

12

French Provencal armoire in walnut.

85

1

2

Queen Victoria

Shakespeare

3

Volunteer Rifle
Corps., jug,
circa 1840.

4

18th century
Staffordshire
duck.

5

Victorian cat.

6

Whieldon green glaze
cradle.

7

19th century
Toby jug.

8

Georgian china
pugs.

9

Lieutenant Hector Munro.

10

Black transfer plate
inscribed Tunstall.

11

PREPARE
TO MEET
THY GOD

Mantelpiece decoration
by Obediah Sherratt, 1820.

12

Whieldon tortoiseshell
teapot.

13

Victorian dogs.

14

19th century
pastil burner.

15

Staffordshire group.

16

CAMPBELL

General Sir Colin
Campbell.

17

Flat back figure.

18

19th century figure.

19

HEENAN SAYERS

'The Boxers' Heenen
and Sayers.

1 Victorian biscuit barrel.

2 A three colour jardiniere.

3 A buff canware jardiniere.

4 Victorian milk jug.

5 Three colour dice pattern teapot.

6 19th century custard cup.

7 19th century hare dish.

8 Blue and white jasper tulip pot.

9 An octagonal teapot.

10 19th century green plate.

11 Green and brown crocus pot, circa 1790.

12 Three colour vase.

13 19th century vase.

14 Blue jasper plaque.

15 Commemorative mug.

16 Rosso Antico pastil burner.

17 A Wedgwood and Bentley variegated creamware urn.

18 Wedgwood and Bentley vase.

19 Three colour dice pattern vase and cover.

1 First period sauceboat.

2 Yellow ground first period basket.

3 A Worcester sauce jug.

4 First period sparrow beak jug.

5 Early 19th century teapoy.

6 A first period mug.

7 A Flight Barr and Barr sauce tureen and cover.

8 First period plate.

9 An early Worcester blue and white tureen stand.

10 First period blue and white plate.

11 First period mug.

12 An early Worcester mug.

13 First period yellow ground tankard.

14 First period transfer printed mug.

15 Late 18th century mug, circa 1780.

16 18th century vase.

17 Dr. Wall hot water jug.

18 First period vase.

19 Dr. Wall blue scale jug.

CHELSEA

CHINA

1

Early model of a pointer.

2

Chelsea peacock.

3

'La Nourrice' with red anchor mark.

4

An early Chelsea model.

5

White figure of a greyhound dated 1749/50 with Crown and Trident mark in underglaze blue.

6

A 'Hans Sloane' pattern red anchor plate.

7

Chelsea Turkish sweetmeat dish.

DERBY

8

A patchmark sheep.

9

Wine cooler bearing the mark 'Duesbury London 1790'.

10

A blue and brown plate.

11

Early Derby figure.

12

19th century figure.

13

19th century candlestick.

14

19th century model of a shorthorn cow.

15

19th century Derby figure.

CHINA
ROCKINGHAM

1
An early plate.

2
19th century Cadogan teapot.

3
An early pot pourri jar and cover.

PARIAN

4
Victorian Parian figure.

5
19th century Parian figure.

6
Victorian figure.

SEVRES

7
19th century ink-stand.

8
Ormolu mounted vase.

9
Sevres tazza, circa 1840.

10
Ewer and basin painted by Jean Dubois, 1757.

GRECIAN

11
A Chalcidan black figure Amphora 580 - 550 BC.

12
An Attic pottery owl Skphos 5th century BC.

13
A 5th century BC pottery female protome.

14
A late period figure of Neith.

15
A black figure band cup Athens 530 BC.

16
An Attic black figure Kylix 540-530 BC.

17
A 6th century BC green glaze ushabji.

DELFT

1. Dutch Delft pottery cow.

2. Blue and white Southwark Delft mug.

3. English Delft bleeding bowl, 1727.

CHINA

4. An early Delft vase.

BELLEEK

5. 19th century jardiniere.

6. Belleek centrepiece.

7. 19th century lattice work basket.

8. A cherub candelabrum.

DOULTON

9. Brown salt glaze figure of Nelson.

10. Queen Victoria commemorative jug.

11. 19th century vase.

12. Vase by Florence Barlow.

13. 19th century tobacco jar.

14. Royal Doulton jardiniere and stand.

15. 19th century jardiniere stand.

16. Terra-cotta Doulton cat.

17. Water set by Hannah Barlow, dated 1885.

CHINA
CREAMWARE

1 Leeds underglaze blue plate.

2 Black transfer octagonal plate.

3 Leeds creamware seated sphinx, circa 1770.

4 An early Leeds creamware jug.

DRESDEN AND MEISSEN

5 Dresden chocolate cup and cover, circa 1860.

6 18th century Meissen dog.

7 19th century Dresden candelabrum.

BOW

8 Bow figure of Bacchus, 1750.

Early pheasant candlestick.

9 An early Bow plate.

10 A Bow candlestick.

11

SALT GLAZE

12 Salt glaze bear jug, circa 1740.

13 Early salt glaze teapot.

14 Mid 18th century bear jug.

IMARI

15 19th century Imari bowl.

16 Pair of 19th century plates.

CAUGHLEY

CHINA

1

19th century blue
and white jug.

2

Early 19th century
pickle dish.

3

A Victorian Caughley
jug.

MINTON

4

A Minton majolica
pot.

5

Early 19th century
Minton greyhound.

6

Minton vase in the
Pate sur Pate style
by L. Salon.

SUNDERLAND LUSTRE

7

Victorian lustre jug.

8

Sunderland lustre
punch bowl.

9

19th century lustre jug.

ENOCH AND RALPH WOOD

10

Enoch Wood mustard
pot, circa 1805.

11

Enoch Wood bust
of John Wesley.

12

18th century bust
of Minerva.

13

Ralph Wood triple
tree trunk vase,
1790.

PRATTWARE

14

19th century Prattware plate.

15

19th century Prattware vases.

16

A plaque of
George III.

CHINA

1 Nicholas II porcelain urn.

2 19th century blue porcelain vase.

3 An early Baroque figure.

CONTINENTAL

4 A four branch candelabrum marked J.R.

5 Medicine jar, Florentine circa 1480.

6 Capi de Monte group 'The Declaration' by Guiseppe Gricci.

7 Cologne ovoid vase.

8 19th century Sampson figure.

9 A Lunds Bristol cup.

10 Limoges candlestick.

11 Russian porcelain figure by Gardner 1830.

12 A Mennecy Magot figure.

13 A Le Nove group.

14 Brussels faience hen tureen and cover.

15 Brussels faience duck tureen.

16 A Paul I St. Petersburg verriere.

17 A Le Nove pair of figures.

18 A Marseilles faience tureen from the Veuve Perrin factory.

94

1
A 16th century Chinese
Kinrande double gourd
vase.

2
Ming stem
cup,
1426 - 1435.

3
19th century Canton
vase.

4
Ch'ien Lung vase.

5
14th century Ming blue
and white wine jar.

6
A T'ang dynasty
horse.

7
Ch'ien Lung plate.

8
Blue and white Chinese
garden seat.

9
Late 17th century
Arita dragon vase.

10
A T'ang dynasty
jar.

11
Chinese famille
rose plate.

12
Yung Cheng famille
rose plate.

13
An early Chinese
pottery funeral jar.

14
18th century
Chinese porcelain
punch bowl.

15
A Ch'ien Lung ground
Canton fish tank.

16
Chinese ginger
jar.

17
Sung pottery
bottle, AD 1200.

18
Early 19th
century
Chinese vase.

19
An early
Canton vase.

20
A T'ang dynasty
pottery tomb figure.

CHINA

1 19th century lustre jug.

2 A Jacob Petit vase circa 1860.

3 A Benjamin Lunds vase.

MISCELLANEA

4 19th century Copeland and Garrett jug.

5 An early Victorian jug.

6 Late Victorian vase.

7 Victorian biscuit barrel.

8 Early Victorian vase.

9 Royal Dux figure.

10 An early yellow ground junket dish.

11 A Victorian comport.

12 Early Victorian nodding figure.

13 1937 Coronation mug.

14 19th century Goss china.

15 Victorian shaving mug.

16 Victorian bed warmer.

17 19th century feeding cup,

18 Victorian slop pail.

1
An early pot pourri
vase, circa
1765.

2
Rare pear shaped coffee
pot and cover.

3
19th century flower
encrusted vase.

4
English pottery jug dep-
icting Franco Russian
war, 1812.

5
19th century vase.

6
An Admiral Rodney
jug.

7
Small Victorian vase.

8
A Liverpool mug.

9
Victorian chamber pot.

10
'Goat in the Well' plate
by Jeffryes Hamett O'
Neale.

11
19th century blue and
white foot bath.

12
19th century iron-
stone vase.

13
Victorian jug and
basin set.

14
Large Victorian cheese
dish.

15
Victorian
pottery
figure.

16
Early Victorian blue
and white tureen.

17
Victorian blue and white
incense burner.

18
A Newhall teapot.

SILVER
COFFEE POTS

George III coffee pot
London 1795.

Silver coffee pot,
London 1771.

George I plain cylind-
rical coffee pot, 1723.

Chocolate pot,
Newcastle 1732.

Victorian coffee
pot, 1845.

George III coffee pot.

George III pear shaped
coffee pot,London 1766.

George III Scottish
coffee pot,
Edinburgh   1760.

George II coffee pot,
1742.

George III coffee jug,
London 1805.

George II coffee pot,
London 1735.

Swedish coffee pot,
1775.

BEAKERS

Silver beaker, London
1802.

18th century beaker.

Charles II beaker,
London 1676.

18th century Swedish
beaker.

TEAPOTS   **SILVER**

1 Victorian plated teapot.

2 Louis XV pear shaped teapot, 1730 Toulouse

3 George IV melon shaped teapot,1820.

4 William IV melon shaped teapot.London1834.

5 19th century silver teapot.

6 George III flat topped teapot.

7 George III silver teapot, 1818.

8 George I bullet shaped teapot, 1724.

9 George III oval teapot, London 1802.

TEA KETTLES

10 George II spirit kettle, 1754.

11 George II silver kettle and stand, 1745.

12 George II kettle, 1738.

13 George III chinoiserie kettle, 1770.

14 George II silver kettle 1765.

15 Victorian Sheffield plate spirit kettle, 1860.

1 18th century Newcastle tankard.

2 A lidded quart tankard, 1749.

3 George II lidded tankard, London, 1753.

4 St. Petersburg silver gilt tankard, 1855.

5 George II silver tankard, London 1732.

6 A German silver gilt tankard, 1580.

7 George IV tankard.

8 German silver tankard, Luneburg, 1620.

9 Early 18th century lidded flagon.

10 George II flagon, 1737.

11 Irish tankard, 1690.

12 George III pint tankard, Newcastle 1774.

13 George III tankard, London 1805.

14 George III baluster tankard London 1793.

15 Regency period reeded tankard.

16 George III tankard, 1808.

17 A Newcastle tankard, 1774,

18 George III tankard, Newcastle 1788.

MUGS   **SILVER**

Baluster shaped
mug, London1728.

English silver mug
1716.

Christening mug,
Birmingham 1861.

Christening mug,
London 1846.

Queen Anne mug London
1702.

Christening mug,
London 1833.

George II half
pint mug, 1740.

Engraved christening
mug, 1911.

Fine English silver
mug, 1759.

Early George II pint
mug, 1730.

Victorian campagna
shaped christening mug.

George III silver
mug, 1765.

CUPS

Early Victorian silver cup,
London 1860.

A Commonwealth plain
wine cup, London 1681.

A Commonwealth silver
wine cup, London 1655.

Small silver cup,
1917.

A Victorian plated
loving cup.

Silver gilt cup,
1737.

A two handled
cup and cover,
London1674.

Hare's mask stirrup
cup, Birmingham 1809.

101

SILVER BOWLS

1

George III vase shaped sugar basin, London 1816.

2

A silver Montieth bowl, 1717.

3

Silver punch bowl Guernsey, 1700.

4

German silver bowl, Hamburg 1729.

5

Silver gilt presentation bowl.

6

Victorian plated bowl.

7

Hexagonal silver gilt sweet bowl, 1933.

8

Silver rose bowl 1901.

9

Victorian silver sweet bowl.

TUREENS

10

Silver tureen and cover, London 1768-69.

11

Early 19th century soup tureen and cover, 1804.

12

An Italo-French soup tureen and cover, 1762.

13

Russian soup tureen and cover.

14

George III sauce tureen, 1790.

15

George IV tureen and cover.

16

An early Dutch sauce tureen

17

George III soup tureen on paw feet.

18

George III tureen in the Egyptian taste, 1807.

TRAYS AND SALVERS

1 19th century plated salver.

2 A Victorian silver gilt childs plate, 1852.

3 George III salver, London 1796.

4 George III silver snuffer tray, London 1775.

6 George III oval tray.

7 George III silver salver.

5 George IV rectangular salver, London 1824.

8 Victorian plated gallery tray.

COASTERS

9 Sheffield plated coaster, 1808.

10 Silver coaster, 1929.

11 George IV silver coaster, London 1825.

12 George III coaster, London 1798.

13 George III pierced coaster, 1784.

14 George III silver coaster with grape and leaf edging.

ENTREE DISHES

15 Victorian plated breakfast dish.

16 Early 19th century entree dish and cover, 1819.

17 George III silver entree dish.

103

SILVER FLATWARE

1. Early Georgian silver mote spoon.

2. marrow scoop, 1837.

3. George II marrow scoop spoon, Dublin 1735.

4. James I Apostle spoon.

5. Silver Apostle spoon, London 1909.

6. Silver punch ladle, London 1790.

7. Early Georgian cast silver mote spoon.

8. Victorian sifter spoon.

9. Charles II trifid lace back spoon, 1683.

10. George III Irish bright cut sauce ladle, Dublin 1790.

11. George II shell back basting spoon, 1736.

CADDY SPOONS

12. Round bowl caddy spoon, 1807.

13. George III caddy spoon Birmingham 1813.

14. Plain caddy spoon Birmingham 1810.

15. Shovel shaped caddy spoon, Birmingham 1819.

16. Thistle top caddy spoon.

17. Jockey cap caddy spoon, 1798.

18. Bright cut V end caddy spoon, 1790.

19. Silver gilt Victorian caddy spoon, 1845.

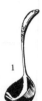

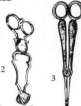

1

Early 19th century silver ladle, 1811.

George III sugar nips, 1750.

Victorian grape scissors, 1865.

19th century scissors.

Cast silver sugar tongs, 1775.

6

Silver sifter spoon London 1838.

BRANDY WARMERS

Silver brandy warmer, 1937.

8

Victorian plated brandy warmer.

9

Early 19th century silver brandy warmer.

CONDIMENTS

10

George IV drum mustard pot, London 1823.

11

George III silver salt cellar, London 1768.

12

George III oblong silver salt cellar.

13

Early Victorian silver salt cellar, 1840.

14

George III silver gilt salt cellar, 1810.

15

19th century mustard pot, 1855.

16

George III mustard pot 1813.

17

George III silver mustard pot 1803.

18

Early 19th century salt cellar, 1810.

SILVER TEA CADDIES

George III silver tea caddy with fluted top and base.

1

2

Set of three silver tea caddies.

3

Victorian silver tea caddy, 1890.

4

Early George III engraved silver tea caddy.

5

Silver tea cannister, circa 1720.

6

Late Georgian plated tea caddy.

INKSTANDS

7

George III silver inkstand with a lace shade.

8

Victorian plated inkwell.

9

George IV silver inkstand.

10

Sheffield plate inkstand, circa 1820.

11

George III silver boat shaped inkstand, 1788.

12

George III boat shaped inkstand, 1795.

BASKETS

13

A silver basket, circa 1796.

14

A Victorian silver cake basket, 1865.

15

Pierced sweet basket 1844.

106

CRUETS

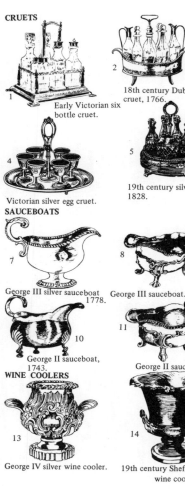

Early Victorian six bottle cruet.

18th century Dublin cruet, 1766.

Victorian egg cruet in the form of a broody hen, 1865.

Victorian silver egg cruet.

19th century silver cruet., 1828.

George III silver cruet, 1799.

SAUCEBOATS

George III silver sauceboat 1778.

George III sauceboat.

Plain George III silver sauceboat, 1794.

George II sauceboat, 1743.

George II sauceboat.

Early Georgian sauceboat.

WINE COOLERS

George IV silver wine cooler.

19th century Sheffield plated wine cooler.

George III silver gilt wine cooler.

SILVER VASES

Victorian silver vase, 1860.

Late Victorian silver vase.

Art Nouveau silver vase, 1910.

CASTERS

Silver sugar caster, 1716.

Silver caster, London 1807.

Silver pepper caster, 1911.

George III sugar caster.

Victorian silver sugar caster.

CLARET JUGS

Edwardian silver mounted glass claret jug.

Victorian silver wine jug, 1885.

Webb cameo glass claret jug.

19th century glass and silver plated claret jug.

19th century claret jug with a silver plated top.

Edwardian plated claret jug.

Victorian claret jug with plated mounts.

1

A William and Mary
silver ewer, 1690.

2

An Elizabeth I
tiger ware jug.

3

George III silver
water jug.

4

George II silver
bell jug, 1751.

5

George II silver
jug, 1730.

6

Queen Anne helmet
shaped ewer, 1702.

7

Victorian plated
cream jug.

8

Silver milk
jug, 1786.

9

George III cream
jug, London 1768.

10

George II Channel
Islands hot milk
jug, Guernsey, 1740.

11

18th century
beer jug.

12

Silver gilt mounted
frosted glass wine jug
1856.

TANTALUS

13

Early 19th century
plated decanter.

14

19th century tantalus with
three cut glass bottles.

15

19th century decanter
stand with cut glass
bottles.

109

SILVER CANDLESTICKS

1 George III loaded candlestick.

2 19th century Sheffield plated candlestick.

3 George III silver gilt candlestick, 1787.

4 19th century Corinthian column candlestick.

5 Queen Anne candlestick.

6 George III candlestick.

7 Sheffield plated candlestick, 1820.

8 Dutch candle stick, 1786.

9 George II tablestick, 1749.

10 Early Georgian silver candlestick.

11 Victorian plated candlestick.

12 Stuart candlestick.

13 George III two branch candlestick.

14 Victorian plated candelabrum.

CHAMBERSTICKS

15 George IV chamberstick 1828.

16 Queen Anne silver chamberstick.

17 George III chamberstick, 1801.

18 George III silver chamberstick.

19 Sheffield chamberstick 1839.

20 George III chamberstick, 1770.

110

MISCELLANEA

SILVER

1 Victorian plated egg steamer.

2 Victorian plated syphon holder.

3 Victorian silver frame.

4 Silver bronze and gilt bust.

5 Victorian silver smokers companion.

6 Italian casket shaped foot warmer, 1730.

7 Victorian silver purse.

8 19th century silver snuff box.

9 Victorian silver group, Birmingham 1861.

10 Russian Faberge silver gilt and enamel kovsh.

11 Late 18th century silver plate warmer.

12 Victorian silver posy holder.

13 George I silver chamber pot.

14 Victorian silver nurses buckle.

15 George III wine label. SHERRY

16 George IV silver and coral rattle, 1827.

17 A George III silver bell.

18 Silver napkin ring, 1910.

19 A Victorian plated tea urn.

20 Victorian silver servers.

111

1

2
Louis XV mother of pearl encrusted snuff box, Paris 1759.

19th century snuff box, 1825.

3
William IV snuff box, London 1836.

4
19th century vinaigrette, 1832.

5
George III nutmeg grater.

6
A Victorian skull pill box.

7
Victorian vinaigrette 1878.

8
Victorian snuff box, 1844.

9
Russian silver gilt and enamelled card case.

10
George III engine turned snuff box, 1803.

11

19th century Dutch silver snuff box.

12
Victorian scent flask in the form of an onion.

13
Victorian silver box.

14
George III vinaigrette.

15
Victorian vinaigrette, Birmingham 1840.

16
Victorian silver match case.

17
19th century silver match case.

18
Silver sovereign case, Birmingham 1902.

1

Vaseline glass scent bottle.

2

Double ended blue overlay scent bottle with silver tops.

3

Blue gilt and enamel scent bottle with gilt top.

4

Victorian ruby glass scent bottle.

5

Victorian double ended ruby glass scent bottle.

6

Art Nouveau cameo glass scent bottle.

7

Blue, gilt and enamel decorated scent bottle.

8

Victorian Bohemian glass red and white overlay scent bottle, 1860.

9

Silver egg scent bottle with a glass stopper.

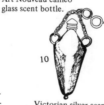

10

Victorian silver scent bottle.

11

19th century engraved silver scent bottle.

MULLS

12

Scottish snuff mull with silver decoration.

13

Victorian silver horn vinaigrette.

14

Georgian snuff mull.

113

SNUFF BOTTLES

1. A Soochow agate bottle.

2. Interior painted snuff bottle.

3. Interior painted snuff bottle.

4. A Peking glass snuff bottle with red floral overlay.

5. Chinese snuff bottle.

6. Floral overlay snuff bottle.

7. Interior painted snuff bottle.

8. Mother of pearl snuff bottle.

9. Interior painted snuff bottle.

10. Hollowed jade snuff bottle.

11. Interior painted snuff bottle.

12. Chinese snuff bottle.

13. Porcelain snuff bottle.

14. Chinese overlay snuff bottle.

15. Chinese snuff bottle.

16. White glass snuff bottle with red overlay.

17. Hornbill snuff bottle with a Rhodenite stopper.

18. Hornbill snuff bottle.

19. An early red overlay snuff bottle.

20. Interior painted snuff bottle.

21. Interior painted snuff bottle.

1
18th century wine glass.

2
Williamite wine glass.

3
English opaque twist ale glass.

4
Crystal glass goblet, circa 1800.

5
Dutch engraved Newcastle glass.

6
English Jacobite wine glass.

7
Newcastle, engraved wine glass.

8
Early English wine glass.

9
Baluster stem wine glass.

10
Newcastle glass.

11
Cotton twist ale glass 1770.

12
Drawn trumpet bowl glass.

13
Victorian coloured wine glass.

14
18th century ribbon twist wine glass.

15
English opaque twist glass.

16
18th century funnel bowl wine glass.

17
Baluster wine glass with a trumpet bowl.

18
Baluster wine glass.

19
A double ogee bowl wine glass.

20
Newcastle wine glass.

21
Engraved wine glass.

22
18th century engraved wine glass.

23
18th century wine glass.

24
18th century fluted bowl wine glass.

25
Tear drop stem wine glass 1740.

115

GLASS

1
Art Nouveau glass
inkwell.

2
Victorian coloured glass bowl.

3
A milk glass crimped
bowl.

4
Glass bowl by Gabriel
Argy - Rousseau.

5
Bristol glass finger
bowl.

6
Victorian opal glass
vase.

7
Victorian slag ware
jug.

8
Mary Gregory glass
pitcher.

9
Cranberry glass jug.

10
Cranberry glass water
jug.

11
Victorian watering
glass.

12
Sunderland Bridge
engraved decanter.

13
Victorian cut glass
centrepiece.

14
Cut glass boat shaped
bowl.

15
Early Georgian wine
bottle.

16
George III plain
glass decanter.

17
Early 19th
century cut
glass decanter.

18
18th century green
bottle.

19
Mary Gregory
dimpled decanter.

20
Late Georgian
decanter,
1780.

GLASS

1 Victorian carnival glass bowl.

2 Bowl by Francois - Emile Decorchemont.

3 Late 19th century coloured glass bowl.

4 Victorian amber glass bowl.

5 Victorian glass bowl.

6 Blue Bristol glass hunting horn, 1820.

7 Georgian cut glass water jug.

8 Burmese glass jug.

9 Cranberry glass jug.

10 A Lutz glass jug.

11 Victorian glass rolling pin.

Land ahoy

12 Blue Bristol gin decanter, 1800.

GIN

13 A Victorian glass pickle jar.

14 George III silver gilt epergne, London 1806.

15 19th century green glass wine bottle.

16 Georgian decanter.

17 Early Victorian overlay decanter.

18 Late 17th century English glass decanter jug.

19 Late Victorian painted decanter.

20 Late Georgian square cut glass decanter.

117

GLASS

1
Cameo glass vase by George Woodall.

2
19th century ruby glass fruit and flower epergne.

3
18th century Bristol five bottle cruet.

4
Victorian red glass lustre.

5
Egyptian bottle, 400 BC.

6
A multi coloured Victorian glass vase.

7
19th century Victorian red glass spill vase.

8
Victorian satin glass vase.

9
Victorian glass spill vase.

10
19th century carnival glass vase.

11
Bohemian gilded glass vase.

12
19th century Tiffany vase.

13
19th century Cranberry glass vase.

14
An early English flute glass.

15
Rare Sidonean bottle, circa 100 AD.

16
Mamluk enamelled glass sweetmeat jar and cover.

17
A translucent green Roman glass flask.

18
A Thomas Webb vase.

118

1

18th century amber flash beaker by Kothgasser.

2

18th century Bohemian double overlay beaker.

3

Amber coloured beaker with a view of Ebergassing by Anton Kothgasser.

4

Amber flash beaker by Kothgasser.

6

7

8

9

5

Victorian satin glass fruit and flower epergne.

Tiffany glass inkwell.

Victorian amber glass spill vase.

Victorian opal glass vase.

Scent bottle by Tiffany.

10

Early Egyptian grave ware tear bottle.

11

19th century red glass spill vase.

12

Victorian opal glass vase.

13

Decorative female figure by Lalique.

14

Chinese overlay vase of the Ch'ien Lung period.

15

A Mamluk enamelled glass Mosque lamp.

16

A Mildner tumbler.

17

19th century Bohemian glass flask.

18

Victorian glass biscuit barrel.

COPPER AND BRASS

1 An early copper frying pan.

2 17th century bell metal skillet.

3 Copper skillet with iron handle.

4 Large 19th century copper pan.

5 Victorian brass preserving pan.

6 Victorian copper wash boiler.

7 A Westborough bronze skillet.

8 19th century copper jardiniere.

9 Georgian copper saucepan complete with lid.

10 An Art Nouveau copper jug.

11 Victorian copper urn with a brass tap.

12 19th century brass watering can.

13 Georgian brass kettle.

14 19th century brass kettle and stand.

15 Georgian copper kettle.

1 Early Georgian copper skillet

2 Georgian brass saucepan.

3 An unusual brass iron of about 1720.

4 19th century copper chafing dish.

5 18th century copper urn.

6 19th century brass water jug.

7 Early 19th century copper milk pail.

8 Early copper frying pan.

9 Victorian copper utensil.

10 A two gallon copper milk churn.

GALLON

11 Late 18th century one gallon copper measure.

12 19th century four gallon copper measure.

13 19th century copper and brass kettle with stand and burner.

14 Late Victorian brass kettle.

15 Victorian copper samovar.

121

COPPER AND BRASS

1
Large Victorian brass crane.

2
19th century copper grape hod.

3
An early brass mortar.

4
A small bronze howitzer.

5
19th century brass revolving magazine stand.

6
Victorian brass 'Crystal Palace' bird cage.

7
Early 19th century brass fire irons.

8
19th century oak and copper grape hod.

9
Victorian brass trivet.

10
Georgian brass trivet.

11
An early brass tavern footman.

12
A Victorian brass fender.

13
Georgian brass and iron grate.

14
Victorian brass and bevelled glass screen.

15
Victorian brass gong.

1 17th century brass, steel handled warming pan.

2 An early brass sundial.

3 An early Martingale.

4 Late 18th century copper warming pan.

5 Victorian brass standard lamp.

6 An early brass candle holder.

7 Victorian brass cake stand.

8 Edwardian brass cash till.

9 17th century bronze bell.

10 18th century brass trivet.

11 Early 19th century brass trivet.

12 A Victorian brass bird cage.

13 An early brass fire grate.

14 Late 19th century pressed brass fire-screen.

15 Regency period brass basket grate.

123

COPPER AND BRASS

1 Georgian model cannon.

2 Victorian brass jardiniere.

3 Bronze Fleur de Lys pestle and mortar.

4 Victorian brass capstan inkwell.

5 Victorian brass inkstand.

6 Large Continental brass mortar.

7 A Victorian brass letter rack.

8 Georgian model brass mortar.

9 Victorian brass candelabrum.

10 Early 19th century ormolu candelabrum.

11 Georgian brass candlesticks.

12 19th century brass candelabrum.

13 French Empire bronze and ormolu candelabrum, circa 1800.

124

1 An early brass pestle and mortar.

2 An early model of a cannonade.

3 English bronze mortar, circa 1690.

4 An early signal cannon with London proofs.

5 Victorian iron and brass fire dogs.

9 Victorian brass crumb scoop.

6 Victorian brass picture frame.

10 A Victorian brass inkstand.

7 Late Victorian brass vase.

8 A Bidri ware brass vase.

11 An early Dutch brass candlestick.

12 Early Victorian brass candlesticks.

13 19th century seven branch brass candle-sticks.

14 19th century brass twist candlesticks.

15 Regency period brass candelabrum.

BUCKETS AND HODS

1

Victorian barge ware
coal bucket.

2

Late Victorian painted
coal scuttle.

3

19th century copper
log bin.

4

Georgian brass
coal scuttle.

5

19th century Firemans
leather bucket.

6

Early Victorian copper
helmet coal scuttle.

7

18th century brass
bucket.

8

Late Victorian cast
iron coal box.

9

An early brass bound
wooden bucket.

10

A Regency waste
paper basket.

11

Late Georgian brass
coal scoop.

12

18th century copper
coal scuttle.

13

Victorian black
japanned coal box.

14

18th century Dutch brass
cauldron on paw feet.

15

Victorian brass
helmet coal scuttle.

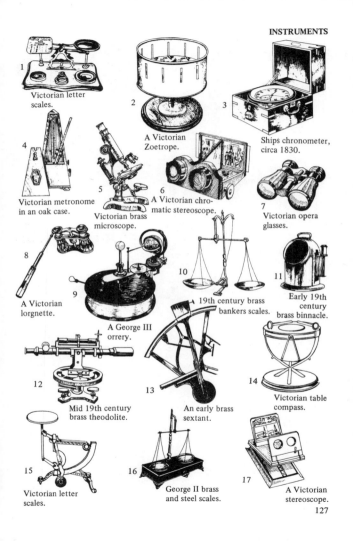

1 Victorian letter scales.

2 A Victorian Zoetrope.

3 Ships chronometer, circa 1830.

4 Victorian metronome in an oak case.

5 Victorian brass microscope.

6 A Victorian chromatic stereoscope.

7 Victorian opera glasses.

8 A Victorian lorgnette.

9 A George III orrery.

10 19th century brass bankers scales.

11 Early 19th century brass binnacle.

12 Mid 19th century brass theodolite.

13 An early brass sextant.

14 Victorian table compass.

15 Victorian letter scales.

16 George II brass and steel scales.

17 A Victorian stereoscope.

127

LAMPS

1 Victorian copper street lamp.

2 Victorian brass oil lamp.

3 A Daum overlay lamp.

4 Victorian brass carriage lamp.

5 Victorian oil lamp with green glass shade.

6 An early Dutch brass lantern, circa 1740.

7 Victorian brass oil lamp.

8 Victorian alabaster and ormolu table lamp.

9 Victorian oil lamp with glass bowl.

10 Victorian ships lamp.

11 Early 19th century witchcraft lamp.

12 A Tiffany lamp.

13 Victorian brass candle lamp.

14 19th century amber glass oil lamp.

15 A bronze and shell lamp by Gurscher.

16 Victorian ships mast lamp.

17 19th century brass table lamp.

18 Victorian sculptured lamp in soft metal.

19 Victorian brass lamp.

20 Victorian brass argand lamp.

1

Early 19th century 'wooden wall' ships lantern.

2

Victorian hanging lamp.

3

Early 19th century copper and steel lantern.

4

Early 19th century six light ormolu chandelier.

5

18th century brass chandelier.

6

A Regency ormolu twelve light chandelier.

7

19th century Continental brass chandelier.

8

19th century cut glass chandelier.

9

Regency period chandelier.

10

An early Continental hanging lamp.

11

Victorian brass hanging lamp.

12

Early 18th century brass chandelier.

13

An early Continental brass hanging lamp.

GRANDFATHER CLOCKS

George III
mahogany
grandfather clock.

An eight day longcase
clock in burr walnut
case.

Mid 18th century oak
case Yorkshire grand-
father clock.

A walnut longcase
clock, London circa
1720.

A late Georgian
regulator clock.

Dutch red walnut
longcase clock,
Amsterdam 1740.

Early 19th century
mahogany eight day
grandfather clock.

18th century longcase
clock with fretted door.

Late 17th century
Dutch marquetry
longcase clock.

Chippendale
figured mahogany
longcase clock.

1

William and Mary
period walnut and
marquetry longcase
clock.

2

George III black and
gold lacquered long-
case clock.

3

Late Georgian brass
faced, oak case, eight
day grandfather
clock.

4

Edwardian oak case
grandfather clock.

5

Early 19th
century
Continental grand-
father clock.

6

Sheraton period
mahogany cased
grandfather
clock.

7

Early 19th century
Continental grand-
father clock.

8

18th century inlaid
longcase clock.

9

French boulle
clock and
pedestal.

10

Late 18th century
mahogany case
grandfather clock
with a painted face.

131

CLOCKS

1

French Regency pedestal clock, circa 1725.

2

Late Victorian black marble mantel clock.

3

Regency period mantel clock.

4

Musical and quarter chiming bracket clock circa 1800.

5

Victorian steeple clock.

6

Early 19th century 'Father Time' clock.

7

Late 18th century Continental brass mantel clock.

8

19th century French lacquered mantel clock.

9

An early porcelain mantel clock.

10

Victorian brass standing clock.

11

Victorian brass mantel clock.

12

Late 18th century ebonised mantel clock.

13

An early Victorian mahogany cased mantel clock.

14

Louis XV Cartel clock in ormolu and tortoiseshell.

15

19th century Dresden striking clock.

16

A Victorian lancet clock.

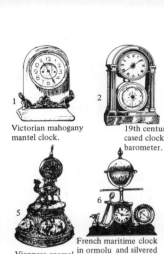

1 Victorian mahogany mantel clock.

2 19th century brass cased clock and barometer.

3 Late Victorian mantel clock.

4 19th century cuckoo clock.

5 Viennese enamel table clock.

6 French maritime clock in ormolu and silvered brass.

7 An early Tabernacle clock.

8 An early 19th century alabaster mantel clock.

9 19th century American beehive clock.

10 A Viennese silver mounted enamel and Lapis Lazuli clock.

11 Empire style white marble mantel clock.

12 French ormolu and tortoiseshell mantel clock.

13 Early 19th century musical clock in a rosewood case.

14 19th century brass mantel clock.

15 French Gothic style mantel clock.

16 19th century American clock in a rosewood case.

133

CLOCKS

1. 19th century French gilt repeat and alarm carriage clock.

2. Victorian brass carriage clock.

3. Eight day French grande sonniere carriage clock.

4. Victorian brass repeater carriage clock.

5. Swiss lever cloisonne cased carriage clock.

6. Late 18th century mahogany bracket clock.

7. Late 18th century bracket clock.

8. Early 19th century repeater carriage clock.

9. Early 18th century bracket clock.

10. Anchor escapement ebonised bracket clock circa 1780.

11. Early 18th century bracket clock with an engraved backplate.

12. A Victorian chiming bracket clock.

13. George III bracket clock.

14. Thomas Tompion silver mounted bracket clock.

15. An early ebonised bracket clock, Edinburgh.

16. An early three train chiming bracket clock, London.

134

1 19th century repeater carriage clock.

2 French brass carriage clock in a shaped case.

3 French carriage clock with alarm and repeater.

4 French carriage clock with pierced and chased case.

5 19th century carriage clock

6 Late 17th century bracket clock.

7 George III bracket clock.

8 French singing bird clock.

Ebony veneered bracket clock by Joseph Knibb.

10 Edwardian bracket clock in a mahogany case.

11 A fine early bracket clock by Edward East 1602 - 1697.

12 Ebonised bracket clock

13 19th century bracket clock in an ebonised case.

14 Late 18th century bracket clock.

15 Mid 19th century ebonised bracket clock.

16 19th century ebonised bracket clock.

CLOCKS

1

A Louis Phillipe
ormolu clock with
Sevres panels.

2

19th century French
mantel clock.

3

19th century French
ormolu eight day clock.

4

French brass archit-
ectural clock,circa
1810.

5

19th century gilded
spelter mantel clock.

6

Early 19th century
ormolu mantel clock.

7

Louis XV ormolu
Cartel clock.

8

Early 19th century
French striking
mantel clock.

9

An early Continental
walnut framed wall
clock.

10

Early 19th century
boulle wall clock.

11

Early 19th century
mahogany cased fusee
movement wall clock.

12

George II
thirty hour
wall clock.

13

Late 18th century mah-
ogany cased Parliament
clock.

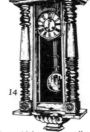

14

Large 19th century wall
clock.

15

Late 19th century
American clock.

136

1
Louis XVI ormolu
clock with Sevres
plaques.

2
Victorian brass
mantel clock.

3
Early German
mantel clock.

4
Early 19th century
ormolu clock with
Sevres plaques.

5
Early 19th century
Brighton Pavilion two
train skeleton clock.

6
19th century
skeleton clock.

7
19th century brass
skeleton clock.

8
Victorian skeleton
timepiece with a
half second dead beat
escapement.

9
An early
Continental
wall clock.

10
A Regency period brass
inlaid octagonal wall
clock.

11
Late Georgian mahogany
cased wall clock.

12
Early 18th
century brass
lantern clock.

13
An unusual transit-
ional lantern clock
with an engraved dial.

14
A Victorian 'Big Ben'
picture clock.

15
An early lantern clock
with anchor escapement.

137

MIRRORS

1 Victorian carved mahogany swing mirror.

2 19th century inlaid mahogany box base toilet mirror.

3 Victorian dressing table mirror.

4 18th century toilet mirror.

5 Victorian gilt gesso mirror.

6 A Hepplewhite mahogany toilet mirror.

7 Louis XVI carved giltwood mirror.

8 Regency period gilt convex mirror.

9 18th century gilt mirror.

10 Late 18th century gilded Adam style wall mirror.

11 Early 19th century Spanish gilded brass bevelled mirror.

12 Late 18th century mahogany wall mirror.

13 Victorian gilded wood mantel mirror.

14 Late 18th century gilt mirror.

15 George II carved giltwood mirror, circa 1740.

16 Late Victorian mahogany cheval mirror.

1 Late Georgian mahogany swing mirror.

2 Late Victorian dressing table mirror.

3 Early Georgian mahogany swing mirror.

4 Early 18th century Chinese lacquer mirror circa 1720.

5 A George II giltwood framed mirror, circa 1750.

6 Queen Anne lacquered toilet mirror.

7 19th century gilded and white painted pine mirror.

8 Georgian giltwood mirror.

9 Late 18th century bevelled glass mirror.

10 An Adam style gilt girandole mirror.

11 Late Georgian rococo style giltwood wall mirror.

12 Chippendale mirror with bird decoration.

13 Late Georgian cheval mirror.

14 Georgian carved and gilded mirror.

15 Late Georgian carved giltwood mirror.

16 Large 19th century gilt wall mirror.

CADDIES AND BOXES

1 Georgian mahogany apothecary box.

2 19th century Dutch tea chest.

3 Victorian writing cabinet.

4 George III mahogany table coaster.

5 19th century pony skin trunk.

6 19th century writers companion.

7 Victorian mahogany cutlery box.

8 Late 18th century knife box.

9 Sheraton mahogany knife box.

10 Victorian parquetry tea caddy.

11 Georgian mahogany cheese coaster.

12 Georgian mahogany cutlery tray.

13 Regency period camphor wood travelling desk.

14 Regency brass bound rosewood toilet box.

15 Sheraton satinwood tea caddy.

16 A Victorian vanity case.

17 Victorian oak smokers companion.

18 19th century mahogany lap desk.

19 Ships Captains Apothecary chest.

1. Regency rosewood tea caddy.

2. Napoleonic prisoner of war straw work box.

3. 19th century games box.

4. 19th century papier mache tea caddy.

5. Victorian biscuit tin.

6. Victorian tortoiseshell tea caddy.

7. Elizabethan oak travelling desk.

8. Victorian burr walnut card case.

9. Early Georgian mahogany tea caddy.

10. Early Victorian tortoise-shell tea caddy.

11. Victorian inlaid mahogany tea caddy.

12. 19th century Tunbridge ware writing slope.

13. Regency rosewood writing slope.

14. Early 19th century inlaid walnut writing box.

15. Regency specimen box.

16. Regency period inlaid rosewood jewel box.

17. Cornelian box with ormolu mounts.

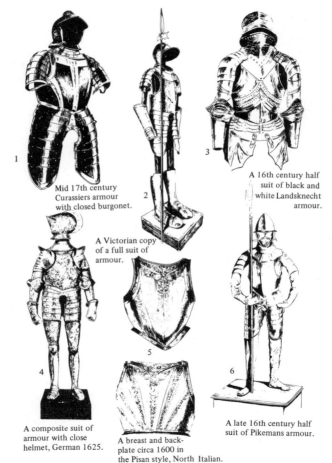

1 Mid 17th century Curassiers armour with closed burgonet.

2 A Victorian copy of a full suit of armour.

3 A 16th century half suit of black and white Landsknecht armour.

4 A composite suit of armour with close helmet, German 1625.

5 A breast and back-plate circa 1600 in the Pisan style, North Italian.

6 A late 16th century half suit of Pikemans armour.

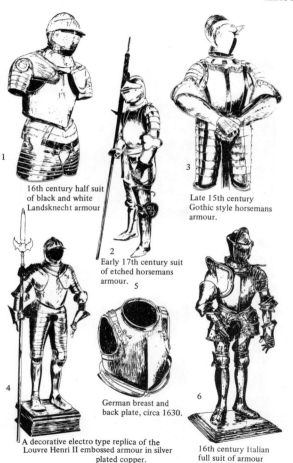

1 16th century half suit of black and white Landsknecht armour

2 Early 17th century suit of etched horsemans armour.

3 Late 15th century Gothic style horsemans armour.

4 A decorative electro type replica of the Louvre Henri II embossed armour in silver plated copper.

5 German breast and back plate, circa 1630.

6 16th century Italian full suit of armour made of bright steel.

MUSICAL BOXES AND AUTOMATON FIGURES

1
An Edwardian phono-
graph, circa 1900.

2
19th century poly-
phone.

3
Late 19th century
gramophone with
a brass horn.

5
Victorian automaton
figure of a Spanish
dancer.

6
19th century autom-
aton figure.

4
A Victorian penny
in the slot polyphone.

7
Late 18th century pipe
organ.

8
An Edwardian record
player.

9
An animated snake
dancer.

10
Victorian musical box.

11
Mid 19th century
musical automaton
group.

12
19th century singing
bird in a cage.

13
Automaton figure of
Pierrot and the Man
in the Moon.

14
Early 19th century
French automaton
group.

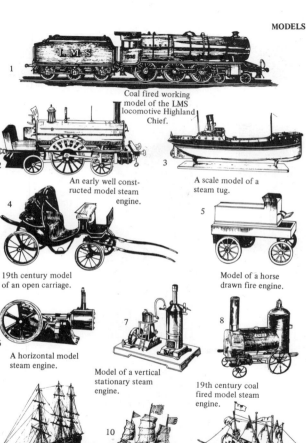

1

Coal fired working model of the LMS locomotive Highland Chief.

2

An early well constructed model steam engine.

3

A scale model of a steam tug.

4

19th century model of an open carriage.

5

Model of a horse drawn fire engine.

6

A horizontal model steam engine.

7

Model of a vertical stationary steam engine.

8

19th century coal fired model steam engine.

9

French Prisoner of War model of the frigate Venus, circa 1815.

10

An Eastern silver model of an armed junk.

11

A Victorian model of a galleon.

1
A Victorian bath chair.

2
19th century barrel topped Romany Vardo.

3
Victorian baby carriage with brass fittings.

4
19th century knife grinders cart.

5
A late Victorian Spider Phaeton.

6
Victorian penny farthing cycle.

7
Late Victorian cart.

8
19th century gig.

9
An early 19th century carriage.

10
Victorian Gypsy Queen caravan.

11
19th century Brougham coach.

12
A two wheel, four seater Governess cart.

13
A late Victorian carriage.

14
An Edwardian Governess cart.

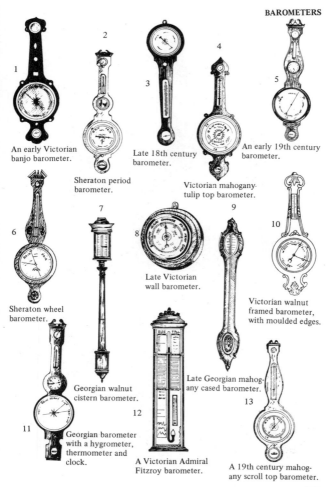

1
An early Victorian banjo barometer.

2
Sheraton period barometer.

3
Late 18th century barometer.

4
Victorian mahogany tulip top barometer.

5
An early 19th century barometer.

6
Sheraton wheel barometer.

7
Georgian walnut cistern barometer.

8
Late Victorian wall barometer.

9
Late Georgian mahogany cased barometer.

10
Victorian walnut framed barometer, with moulded edges.

11
Georgian barometer with a hygrometer, thermometer and clock.

12
A Victorian Admiral Fitzroy barometer.

13
A 19th century mahogany scroll top barometer.

147

DOLLS AND TOYS

1
Victorian doll in a red frock.

2
A Victorian china doll.

3
Small Victorian doll.

4
Doll by Armand Marseille, 1891.

5
A Simon and Halbig doll.

6
Late Napoleon III doll.

7
Victorian doll complete with carriage.

8
A Jumeau doll.

9
A rare French doll stamped Mme. Rohmer.

10
Late 19th century clockwork model engine.

11
Victorian wooden horse drawn caravan.

12
A Victorian dolls house.

13
Late 17th century painted wooden rocking horse.

14
Victorian rocking horse.

15
Victorian model of a railway signal box.

16
An early Victorian wooden pony and trap.

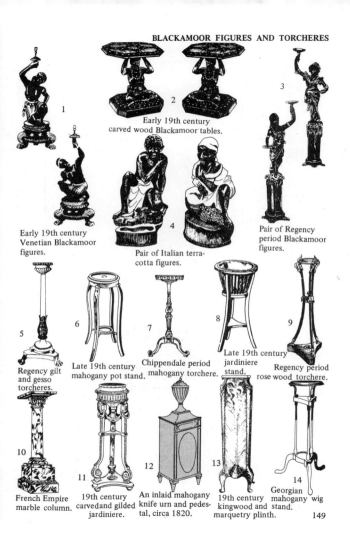

1

2

Early 19th century
carved wood Blackamoor tables.

3

Early 19th century
Venetian Blackamoor
figures.

4

Pair of Italian terra-
cotta figures.

Pair of Regency
period Blackamoor
figures.

5

Regency gilt
and gesso
torcheres.

6

Late 19th century
mahogany pot stand.

7

Chippendale period
mahogany torcheres.

8

Late 19th century
jardiniere
stand.

9

Regency period
rose wood torcheres.

10

French Empire
marble column.

11

19th century
carved and gilded
jardiniere.

12

An inlaid mahogany
knife urn and pedes-
tal, circa 1820.

13

19th century
kingwood and
marquetry plinth.

14

Georgian
mahogany wig
stand.

149

MISCELLANEA

1 19th century two wheel coffee mill.

2 Early 19th century stonebow.

3 Noble shop sign of a horse's head.

4 A Victorian iron work plant stand.

5 19th century marble bust of a Roman Emperor.

6 Scottish spinning wheel.

7 Georgian mahogany Butlers tray.

8 A Georgian mahogany spinet.

9 19th century carved stone heraldic lion.

10 Victorian brass heliograph.

11 19th century papier mache tray.

12 19th century brass telescope.

13 A Charles II walnut baby walker.

14 19th century mahogany and brass binnacle.

15 Late 19th century carved stone fountain.

1

An early cricket bat trolley.

2

Late Georgian library steps.

3

An Italian 19th century carved Carrera marble seat.

4

Victorian cutlery cleaner.

5

An early terra cotta jardiniere.

6

Victorian bamboo hall stand.

7

A wrought iron garden bench dated 1860.

8

Georgian carved stone vase.

9

A mahogany hoddmeter.

10

Regency period terrestrial globe.

11

Coaching Inn sign of Dick Turpin.

12

A mahogany ships wheel.

13

A Flemish two manual harpsichord.

151

MISCELLANEA

1 Bronze mare and foal by Isadore Bonheur.

2 A bronze and ivory group 'Toujours les Amis'.

3 Bronze by C.E. Dallin 'Appeal to the Great Spirit'.

4 A Shang dynasty archaic bronze wine vessel.

5 A Nigerian bronze panthers head mask.

6 19th century bronze figure of a greyhound.

7 Ivory netsuke in the form of a crab.

8 An ivory and shabay-ama elephant.

9 19th century ivory group of a mother and child.

10 Victorian carved ivory figure of a rat.

11 A wood and ivory figure signed Yoshiaki.

12 A finely carved 19th century German ivory tankard.

13 Louis XVI ormolu mounted ivory vase.

152

1

18th century pewter
lidded flagon.

2

18th century pewter
charger.

3

An early 18th century
pewter measure.

4

Victorian pewter
coffee pot.

5

Mid 19th century
Officers sporran of
the 79th Cameron
Highlanders.

6

Victorian model of
a barking Boston
Terrier.

7

Victorian silhouette
in a maple frame.

8

A four case inro.

9

19th century stuffed
bird in a glass case.

10

17th century powder
flask.

11

19th century glass
ship under dome.

12

19th century ceramic
garden seat.

13

Victorian pottery
elephant oil lamp.

14

A shell tree under a
glass dome,
circa 1800.

MISCELLANEA

1

19th century oak
peg tankard.

2

Miniature Victorian
sideboard.

3

A Ch'ien Lung green
jade bowl.

4

Early 19th century
brass sugar cutters.

5

Victorian oak biscuit
barrel.

6

Victorian adjustable
book ends.

7

8

Victorian flat iron.

9

A rock crystal ball.

10

A well formed specimen
of Hematite.

A Scrimshaw whales
tooth.

11

19th century iron
money box.

12

Victorian papier
mache letter rack.

13

A four case inro.

14

Victorian turned
wood tobacco jar.

15

A sawn and polished
Vug.

16

The Infernal Harp shell
from the Fringing Reef,
Mauritius.

17

A French copper
and brass powder
flask.

IN D EX

INDEX

156

INDEX

THE END.

FINEM RESPICE.